SEO & Affiliate Marketing
Playbook

Follow This Step by Step Advanced Beginners Guide For Making Money Online With Search Engine Optimization, Blogging, And Affiliate Marketing; Learn The Secrets NOW!

By Graham Fisher

"SEO & Affiliate Marketing Playbook Follow This Step by Step Advanced Beginners Guide For Making Money Online With Search Engine Optimization, Blogging, And Affiliate Marketing; Learn The Secrets NOW!" Written by "Graham Fisher".

SEO & Affiliate Marketing Playbook is a bundle of the books "The Advanced Affiliate Marketing Playbook", & "SEO Mastery".

Hope You Enjoy!

The Advanced Affiliate Marketing Playbook

Learn Secrets from the Top Affiliate Marketers on How You Can Make Passive Income Online, Through Utilizing Amazon and Other Affiliate Programs Successfully!

By Graham Fisher

Table of Contents

Introduction

Are you new to affiliate marketing? Not sure what it's all about?

Well, affiliate marketing involves marketing products online to get a commission from sales made through your recommendation.

You'll build a website, and place affiliate links to products you are marketing. Then when somebody clicks on your links and purchases a product within a specific time frame, you receive a commission.

There are different affiliate networks that you can register to get products to market.

Affiliate marketing is an excellent business opportunity, and that allows affiliates to get new customers. The business is good for both the company and the affiliate to link up and allow others to buy a product or service.

Affiliate marketing has experienced its downside too, mostly because affiliates don't want to be honest. However, these methods are coming to an end because of the new laws and search engine algorithms.

The hardest category for an affiliate is a newbie. It is hard because as a newbie you need to research for a niche, look for keywords, build a website, choose the best affiliate networks and establish an authority.

As a new affiliate, it is hard, and you can either tell how to make money right away or not. Whichever way, this book is designed to guide you into how you can hit the ground running in affiliate marketing without having to struggle. Anyone can take part in affiliate marketing, but only those who are serious about it make it.

Chapter 1: Getting Started with Affiliate Marketing

Affiliate marketing is a popular method that most people use to make money online. It is a method where a person links up with a business to make a commission by recommending visitors or readers to a particular business service or product. It is one of the oldest methods of marketing. In simple terms, it is defined as a way in which an individual refers another person to an online product or service. Once that person decides to purchase a product based on the recommendations, a commission is earned. The amount of commission varies. For instance, it could range between $1 to $10, 000 depending on the type of product one is marketing.

History of Affiliate Marketing

While affiliate marketing has been around for a very long time, it didn't just start with the invention of the internet though that was the time when it began to take off.

Many people know that affiliate marketing happens online. They believe that a person must have an internet connection to run an affiliate marketing business. In fact, most people only know of the method where you click a link to a product or service, and then the owner of the link receives a small commission for that link click.

However, it can be something different, for example, when you are given a discount by a product owner for directing a new customer to their business. So the person who referred a new customer is given a cut by the product owner in any purchase they make. That is the same thing as referring someone to click a product link. As a product owner, you can also ask your customers how they heard about your product. This can help you to learn where most of your clients originate, but this method will not reveal more information compared to an online system.

For that reason, the coming of the internet has made this marking better and efficient. Businesses have the chance to expand and make more profit. Although the history of affiliate marketing started way before the internet, the internet is credited with making it known to many businesses.

When the web came around, it was a new concept. No one knew that with just a few clicks one could be connected to the whole world. But the internet made this a reality. Traders and retailers did not have to depend on their geographical area to make sales. As long as you had the internet, you could sell to anyone located at any part of the world. For that reason, new marketing strategies had to be developed and applied in many different places in the world. For example, shipping options were introduced.

Patent of Affiliate Marketing

The affiliate marketing patent was awarded to William J. Tobin in 1989. He is the pioneer behind the history of affiliate marketing. He created the first affiliate marketing program for his company PC Flowers & Gifts. This company is known for delivering a large order of flowers around the globe. William created the first framework for what is credited as the history of affiliate marketing. Although it has changed so much, the basic concept is still the same.

The first affiliate networks

In 1998, Click bank and Commission Junction started their business and continued to be among the most popular affiliate networks in the history of affiliate marketing. These networks created the pathway for smaller firms that don't belong to Amazon to join in the affiliate marketing. The merchants were able to pay a small registration fee to sign up for the network and then the network would pay people to use the links to various products. This helped many businesses to expand and allow other people to get paid for helping out with the process. It is a great idea that can be used in many different places.

Up to Date

Nowadays, a lot has changed in the affiliate marketing, but the basic concept is the same. The internet has gone through changes, and it will continue to evolve. But the only way for one to remain at the top is to stay updated and embrace the changes. By remaining updated, it will help you to stay ahead and propel your business.

Current Challenges

In the current world of mobile advertising and business, approximately 90 percent of the advertisers consider affiliate marketing an important component in the general marketing strategy. Affiliate marketing has done well over the years and is still expanding. For one to stand out in the market, one must learn the traits of consumers and learn how to market products.

But the main question is, are you capable of discovering yourself as a potential for affiliate marketing? What are some of the risks and challenges that should be moderated so that they can't affect your journey?

First, it is important to learn to identify the challenges that many businesses face every day and the possible solutions to overcome some of those problems.

We outline for you some of the common challenges that affiliate businesses experience.

- **Selecting the correct niche**

It will be a big problem if you don't get this right. The amount of profit you make from a business will highly depend on finding the correct niche and knowing your interest.

One of the most important things is the choice of your niche. Your market niche will determine how much success you are going to realize. That is why you have to aim at creating a balance between a profitable niche and one that is related to your interests. Many people who engage in affiliate marketing close their business because they can't make enough profit, and end up losing their interest.

As a result, a deep research is inevitable if you want to succeed. Also, you must select a profitable niche and one that you are passionate about.

Finding the right content and compelling copy is a challenge

It is painful to lose customers because you don't have a compelling content. A lot of affiliate business fail because of this reason. It is important to know that customers have a short attention span. For that reason, you must ensure that your website has an attractive content.

The right copy emulates the products and services passively. A captivating content on a website can assist in generating sales. Poor content will impact the SEO and would not reveal the right details of your services.

When you write great content, it will provide your product and services from a different angle. So if you want to be a successful affiliate, you have to take care of the nuances of writing and consider the following issue as a challenge. Your content is a response to their search.

If you think you can't get time to write great content, hire a freelancer to write content for you. Also, SEO and page optimization experts have to be hired. Develop a habit of making use of relevant phrases and proper use of language tools.

- **Generating Targeted Traffic**

It would be hard for you if you can't reach out to the right type of customers. When you don't have a targeted traffic, you will find it hard to make something from the blog.

The only platform for you to enjoy traffic updates is your website. The most common source of traffic is search engines. Traffic can also be generated through Facebook ads, SEO, AdWords, and other social media techniques. But that is still not enough.

There is a difference between visitors who come to your website and the audience you target for your services and product. This will lead to a few unique users but a higher conversion rate. And this will reward you handsomely.

Solution: Optimize your pages and campaigns using the right SEO. Then master your traffic, and you will receive a better insight to help you make more sales. The primary sources that you need to focus are guest blogging, social media, advertising and off-site content marketing that will assist in generating traffic and ranking your pages.

- **Hard to master the basic skills of affiliate marketing**

Running an online business is a great way to earn a living. But it is possible for everything that you have established to crumble down instantly. You can have high traffic and clicks but end up recording zero profits. That is quite possible especially when the links aren't well positioned on your website or even in the mailer content.

Most marketers like to go for a short cut by giving out a copy-paste code which misleads consumers. In case the links aren't placed correctly, the vendors will be directed to the vendor's website, but the referral is not going to be tracked. This way, there will be no sales conversion.

So the best solution is to make sure that you test your affiliate links before you can go live. Ensure that you are familiar with different free resources and websites on the internet that can be helpful in the application of HTML codes and affiliate links.

- **Sustaining Affiliate Business is difficult**

When your business makes some money, that doesn't imply that it will be easy for you to land customers or even keep them for long. One thing with affiliate marketing is that you need to have a large volume of customers. Additionally, your customers must be rich enough to buy your products.

Some of the reasons why you may record low sales include lack of profit and poor conversion rates. But the main issue revolves around the lack of traffic.

Without relevant information to attract customers, people will end up getting stuck in affiliate marketing. Another aspect that should be considered is keyword targeting. It is essential to factor in the intention of the search using keyword phrase. Here, you should try to use different analytical tools to help you identify the problems.

In general, it is up to you to highlight where the problem could be, whether it's poor traffic or low conversion rate. Think about your problem, revisit and review your marketing strategies.

How Affiliate Marketing engine operates

To those of you who are new to affiliate marketing, it may look like a black box. The internal working may appear odd to marketers, and in many firms, it is not given the same focus like other channels. Some affiliate marketers are only aware of the bad reputation accorded by industry players in the 2000s, so they consider it a spam. But the truth is complicated. Even though affiliate programs can have avenues for off-brand promotion, if it is done correctly, they can generate between 5-15 percent of online revenue. In addition, they can have the highest ROI among any online channel. For that case, CMOs have discovered that affiliate marketing can be a great tool in their business. That is why they decided to integrate the system into their marketing methodologies.

The performance results measure affiliate marketing. In other words, affiliates only receive payment when their efforts in promotion lead to a transaction.

Affiliates

Affiliates can include a different type of website, but in most cases, they are bloggers or sites linked to the merchant's industry. The role of affiliates is to reveal to visitors the products of the merchant. They can do this by writing blog posts associated with the new product or promotions on the merchant's site.

Traditionally, most affiliate programs feature coupon codes and loyalty sites. When an industry grows, content bloggers continue to occupy the best place in many programs. Creative programs also define an affiliate, even more, they collaborate with individual professionals, schools and nonprofits.

Payments

One reason why affiliate marketing has a better ROI than other marketing channels is that of the performance measurement. The merchants can only pay for the original customers. This provides affiliate marketing with an upper hand than streams such as PPC, where it is easy for one to spend most of the money on clicks without building an initial conversion.

When we have many affiliates participating in a particular transaction, the payments become complex. Sometimes, it is possible for an affiliate to get commission for customers introduced by other affiliates. Successful programs take advantage of multi-channel attribution to ensure that affiliates create the best value.

Networks

Affiliate programs have different structures. In addition, they have different affiliate networks. Some networks collaborate with multiple networks while some are consolidated into one. Most affiliates work on different networks.

The network has cookies to track the progress of the customer from affiliate website through the merchant shopping cart. The network can automatically pay commissions to affiliates depending on the rules set by the merchant.

Management

Merchants can control affiliate programs in-house while others can turn the management to their affiliate network. Whoever controls the program implements the function of affiliates, involve them, and discover the methods used to market the merchant and the value that reveals incremental revenue.

Affiliate Marketing Vs. Traditional Ecommerce

Launching an online business is something that most people dream to do. An online business can provide one with a lot of freedom. For example, you choose when to report to work and when to close and go back home. In other words, you are the CEO of your own business. Most people who own an online business prefer to work from the comfort of their home. Other people rent a small office, and others decide to work as they travel across the country.

If you are already reading this, the chances are that you are familiar with the many benefits that come with being an online entrepreneur. The biggest challenge that you could be facing is twofold. Maybe you want to know how can you start an online business and what type of business can you start although there are many different kinds of online business that you can begin. This section will deal with whether you need to start e-commerce or affiliate marketing.

Difference between affiliate marketing and E-commerce

Typically, as an affiliate marketer, you would be marketing and selling products and services. By doing so, you will earn some commission for each service or product you sell. But an e-commerce business is different. For the e-commerce business, you sell your own products and services.

Additionally, you are the one who will set the prices for each product so that you can make a profit on each product you sell. One thing with choosing to run an e-commerce business, you have the option to incorporate affiliate marketers so that they can market your business. In general, both kinds of businesses have advantages and disadvantages. We shall discuss each in the next section.

Advantages of beginning a traditional e-commerce business

Before you can launch your own e-commerce business, you must ensure that you do an in-depth planning. But you must remember that it is not easy to start an e-commerce business. The best thing is that you don't need to be an inventor or creator of a product. Most online promoters will create their own courses for sale or even as a platform for them to sell an e-book. Some e-commerce owners may choose to stock their store and engage drop shippers to help ship their products. Others may decide to buy specific niche products in bulk; this will give them a chance to sell the products on their website at a particular cost.

Essentially, the most significant advantage that comes with starting an e-commerce business compared to affiliate marketing is the freedom you get regarding promotions, pricing, and acquiring new customers. When a person buys directly from you, you have the opportunity to get their names, phone numbers, addresses, and everything that you need to facilitate a repeat business. Additionally, you can develop a better idea of how you can price products for the best profits and define the right way to market your products. You will never have to deal with an affiliate manager, set up prices that you can't control, limitations on the type of advertising you can apply, or bad affiliate contracts. Everything is up to you, and that is a great benefit.

E-commerce is a type of business that can be scaled up fast compared to the affiliate marketing business. In case you succeed in e-commerce, you can always expand your business by looking for advertising methods that have a higher ROI and repeat customers who can come back to buy.

Disadvantages that come with E-commerce business

There is a high risk and more financial investment involved in starting an e-commerce business. For example, if your goal is to be a reseller by buying bulk items from China and reselling them on your website for a specific profit, you may need to purchase enough of the product before you meet the threshold of the bulk price. This means that you must store your product in a different place and identify a method to pick, pack and ship the product once you have sold it. You are also supposed to set up payment processing platforms, deliver customer service, accept refunds, returns, and control your day-to-day operations. This can be time-consuming and stressful, especially for new entrepreneurs.

Merits of Affiliate Marketing

Affiliate marketing has many advantages. Since you will be selling and promoting other people's services, there is no need to be scared of customer service, sales taxes, payment processing, warehousing, shipping product or even any other time-consuming features of selling your own products. All that you have to do is to create a link to people's products and services. When a person clicks on your affiliate links and purchases a product, you can receive between 5% to 75% commission. You can even have affiliate partners that can pay you 75% commissions. There are also many products and services that you can promote that deal with every niche, so you will have a lot to choose from.

Another great advantage to affiliate marketing is the low barrier to entry. The startup costs are a bit low; this makes it a great option for everyone. Whatever you need is the ability to create an exciting website.

What is the best to go for?

If you are a new affiliate marketer, it is important to start with affiliate marketing. By starting with affiliate marketing, you can dig deep into online marketing without entering into any risk. If you can make it in affiliate marketing and sell products and services, there will be no reason why you can't succeed in e-commerce. However, everyone is advised to test and learn by selling products before you can dive into an online business.

Ultimately, your end goal is to have a business that generates profits from both affiliate marketing and e-commerce. All in all, when you run an affiliate marketing business, it will give you the time to focus on what you love to do and help people make buy the best products and access the right service decisions.

How profitable is Affiliate Marketing

The most common question for anyone who wants to start affiliate marketing is whether it is a profitable business. The short answer is yes. A detailed explanation is that one has to consider several factors. If your goal is to join affiliate marketing and make huge profits with minimal effort, the chances are that you will come out very disappointed.

That should not make you think like affiliate marketing is difficult, but you need to have some knowledge. You must have a good plan and remain consistent.

Other factors that you must put into consideration include:

- Select only quality services and products. Also, make an effort to buy them before you can promote them. Remember that your followers will develop a first impression of you based on the type of products you will be promoting.

- Perform research about the affiliate programs to learn about the mode of payment. This type of research will allow you to be certain about the program.

- Track success of your affiliate programs. You can decide to use an affiliate tracking software. This kind of software will help you especially when you are using different affiliate programs.

- Go for products that aren't very popular, but ensure that they are products that you are passionate about. It is important in this case to gather information about products from another niche, and how the problem experienced by users of the products are resolved.

To make profit in affiliate marketing, you have to spend time and do quality research on how you can make your business successful. The most important thing for starters is that affiliate marketing is not a quick and effortless method to earn income. There is no get rich quick scheme. You must have the right plan and correct implementation of the said plan for you to be profitable in the affiliate marketing.

The realities of affiliate Marketing-Crucial insights for starters

As previously mentioned, affiliate marketing is a bit complex. Like any other means that produces revenue, success in this sector comes with the effort you put in and the consistency. The reality is that affiliate marketing can be a fantastic home business that doesn't need much capital to launch, and you don't need to have a fixed cycle of revenue. No need to deliver a service.

The main problem with affiliate marketing like any other home-based job option is the wrong ideology that one can become a millionaire in an overnight with little effort. You may have come across claims that you can make thousands of dollars in a month by just clicking links. Some have even gone on to say that you could set up your own affiliate site and wait to check your bank deposits to find out how much you have made.

That is false. The truth with affiliate marketing is that there is no shortcut to become rich. A few people who have made huge earnings from affiliate marketing have invested most of their efforts and time. Also, they have worked correctly in implementing their strategies. So the question that you need to ask yourself today is not whether or not it is a genuine way of earning income, but whether or not you can turn this into a right choice given your abilities and skills. That decision is left for you to make.

Drawbacks of affiliate marketing

Some of the challenges to keep in mind before deciding to start affiliate marketing include:

- It can take some time for one to generate a given level of traffic to your pages which will possibly lead to better income.

- There is the risk of affiliate hijacking.

- You are only responsible for a referral, and there is no control over the service or product and how they carry out the business with your references.

- Certain companies don't pay affiliates. That is why you have the option to research the affiliate programs and discover the most reliable ones.

- There is high competition. If you find an excellent program to participate, you should know that there is an excellent number of affiliates who want to promote the same.

Chapter 2: Products of Affiliate Marketing

Digital Products

Affiliate programs in the digital products category include products and services found online. These include new offers that are available for purchase or are downloadable and shippable to the customer's front door.

Additionally, it's hard to find via a network. Digital products don't have many different links and banners for one to choose from. Instead, there is a single link that redirects to the landing page for a customer to transact. Examples of digital products include eBooks, MP3, PDFs, website themes, software, and graphics. There is an extensive collection of things to choose from, such as PDF Guides, WordPress plugins, learning programs like Udemy, video game downloads, online universities and many more. Digital products sell very high, so you should expect to receive big commissions.

Physical Products

These are products that one can purchase at a Wal-Mart or a different retailer. They are merchandise, apparel, and other physical goods that one can sell and ship to customers.

Pros and Cons of Digital and Physical Affiliate Products

Nowadays, millions of people buy products that are only found online. Most of these products are digital. The sales of digital products like audiobooks, eBooks, online courses, and software have risen.

The eBook market is expected to increase to 16% by 2021. That stat shows how digital products are rising in the market. According to ClickBank, the last 20 years has experienced a rise in demand for digital products, which help buyers solve their problems.

Some affiliate marketers concentrate only on digital products. Others focus on physical products, and some decide to take advantage of both digital and physical products. Below are advantages of each product.

The Pros

Digital affiliate products provide the following advantages.

- **High Commission**

Physical products have a higher advertising cost. The advertiser will have to pay for the ingredients, warehousing costs, packaging, and shipping costs.

- **No shipping restrictions**

Digital products don't have any restrictions. In fact, they are immediately available to customers. For the physical products, the little bits of the product have to be carefully considered before they can pass in the customs.

Additionally, there must be a reliable way of shipping. But digital products carry none of these requirements. As long as the customer has free access to the internet and a means of payment, they can proceed with the purchase.

- **Instant delivery**

Once a customer purchases a digital product. The product is made available for them to download. It is useful to the customer and the affiliate. Customers may be tempted to make an impulse buy especially when they know that they get the product instantly. Since customers read pre-sell descriptions, that will convince them that the product is the correct one, so they will be confident to get started and see the results.

- **Convenience**

For the case of e-book affiliates, one of the advantages that it provides is convenience. Instead of customers searching online to look for all the information, they will prefer to purchase a product that has all the reliable information in one source. E-book writers gather all the required information into a single document that is easy to read.

The Cons

Besides the advantages that one gets with digital products, there are also disadvantages related to digital products. Some of these disadvantages include:

- **Information is free**

Content marketers spend a lot of time to write informative articles and advice that they can give away for free so that they can attract visitors to their websites. A lot of information is freely available online, and that may discourage you from creating your digital product. Well, the success of ClickBank originates from delivering to visitor's unique products. That means if you focus on delivering products with the right benefits, you'll never lack customers.

- **Quality concerns**

Potential customers can be worried about the standards of the digital product and whether it is worth the money they have paid for. Why? Anyone can create a digital product because there is no high capital needed for one to become an eBook vendor. As a result, there are chances that a product can be of low quality. In addition, there is a perception that physical products are more worth than digital products.

To solve this problem, ensure that you pick an excellent digital product. Sometimes, you can judge how good a product may be based on how well it is designed. If a product is well-designed and it appears like the owner spends time to create it, that will automatically convince the buyer.

A tip that successful eBook sites use is to create product images that look like a real physical book. Although the visitor knows that they are buying a digital download, it will make the visitor believe that it is worth.

Similarly, having a website is important in building trust. If you have a well-designed website with an "about section" and active social media pages, it will reassure potential customers that they will get a quality product in exchange for their money.

Also, a potential customer will be interested in what's found inside a product. Try to see whether you can find a sample product to give you a better understanding of what's included, and how well researched and designed it is.

You can decide to share a brief of the contents or even some screenshots.

- **No reorders**

With physical products, there is some hope that the customer can come back to purchase the same product. E-books are different, once a customer buys it, they won't return to buy it. However, you will receive benefits from upsells and cross-sells where the customers provide extra products.

- **Higher return rates**

Sometimes, customers may want to buy a digital product at an impulse because there are few obstacles to prevent them from returning the product. But when they find a product is of great quality and matches whatever was in the pre-sell, there will be low percentage of return.

Products that have money-back guarantee can also reduce the rapid change in mind in the customer because they know that they can return it in a given period and get a full refund.

How to find the Best products to promote?

You can make a good profit in affiliate marketing as long as you maintain the commitment levels. When you start your online business, the right way to get immediate results is to begin by marketing other people's products in return for a commission. Below are some things that you should consider:

Know your passion

Affiliate marketing is a great platform for one to make profit, but how can one identify the best products to promote? Let's assume you already have your blog set up, and you want to start to receive the benefits of affiliate marketing. First, you must know your passion. Don't decide to do something just because you want to earn money. The chances are that it will not succeed in the long-term. For that reason, it is important to market something that you have interest in. So start by researching for products that you use. That way you can be sure to write from a firsthand experience.

Successful affiliates promote products that they are passionate about. As a result, choose your niche.

Look for an industry that you want to invest your affiliate business.

You can select an industry depending on the level of passion and where you believe you can dedicate all your effort. A potential customer can tell from your marketing copy whether you have interest in that product or not.

Play to the rules of the game

Let's imagine that you have a real estate blog, and you try to sell pet care products in your affiliate program, the chances are that it is not going to work. That is why you need to customize your products to things that people come to your blog would be interested in.

But before you can implement anything, it is important to do some research about your target market. The biggest mistake that people make is to judge the probability of success based on what someone else did. To ensure that you don't do the repeat the mistake, speak with your target customer base.

As an affiliate marketer, you must have a list of your potential customers. Regardless of the type of product you select, you want to make sure that you don't experience any problem in marketing. You must feel safe and confident to recommend it so that you don't destroy your reputation.

You can use Google Trends to help you identify the type of products you want to market. It will also help you to monitor the search volume of keywords. It is a great way to verify how well the products in your niche sell.

Stick with the virtual products

Next, you must decide whether you want to promote digital or physical products. It is your role to identify the kind of products that will generate more profits and offer benefits.

Digital products have more benefits for physical products. Also, they are much easy to market than physical products. For example, there are shipping expenses. And once the payment is made, the clients receive a link to download the product.

In other words, there is a less hassle, worry, and you can never run out of stock.

Begin with ClickBank

The easiest way to find the best products to market online is by registering with an affiliate marketing site like ClickBank. ClickBank will provide you with thousands of products to market in any niche. The commission ranges between 50-75%, with a better price tag.

They have a large collection of electronic products to pick, and they support different payment methods. As such, you are sure to receive your payment on time. ClickBank also provides a real-time reporting for all their products.

One of the best features with ClickBank products is Gravity. This feature allows you to see how the number of affiliates selling for a given product. The higher the number, the more people selling it. But you should avoid products with 100+ Gravity because that is a highly competitive industry.

Choose products that have at least 20 people promoting it. This shows that the product has a sales rate that converts well and is trusted by marketers.

Next, look for products that are not very cheap or expensive. A low-cost product may help cut down the value of the product. On the other hand, a high price may result in low sales.

Regarding the number of products to market, you can start with one. Focus on that one, research and learn the different strategies to be successful. Apply those strategies and slowly expand your business.

Lastly, ensure that you search for products that serve people and solve their problems. Your products should solve their problems. Use these tips to find the best products to market online. Remember. Your ultimate success in affiliate marketing depends on each product you decide to market and how you can market its features so that customers can trust its benefits.

Best Products to Promote on Amazon

If you really want to make passive income from Amazon, this section reveals to you a collection of Amazon products that you can market as an affiliate. These are hot Amazon products that if you implement your marketing strategies correctly, you will make some good profit as an affiliate.

Some affiliates make huge commissions from selling expensive products. The only problem is that some of these products don't have high volume sales. Therefore, you must take time to research products that have high sales volume and are expensive.

A secret for you

Most online consumers buy solutions but not product. That means you must look for problems that affect people and offer solutions in the form of products.

Again, you must know why people would want to spend money on the product you market. And the secret is to know the problems that your customers go through. Then for you to make money, you must offer a suitable solution to address that problem. The best thing about this is that you don't have to sell to them, but they'll willingly buy it without you convincing them.

Why? Everybody wants to solve their problems regardless of the amount of money it is going to cost them.

Mountain Bikes

Mountain bikes are very popular with a lot of innovations released that reflect a rapidly growing market. With new changes in design, handling, and durability. This is a great market worth to try out. Some of the sites dedicated to reviewing mountain bikes include:

- Bicycling.com

- Outdoorgearlab.com

- Outsideonline.com

Car Covers

The latest car covers have been designed to be thick for full protection. Most feature reflective top layers to protect against the sun and rain. Since many people own a classic car, car covers can be popular in winter. If you would like to read the best car covers review. Below are a few sites to look out for.

- Carcover.com

- Carcoverstore.com

- Autoaccessoriesgarage.com

Motorcycle Helmets

Motorcycle helmets are advanced than ever before with unique pull-down visors, cooling vents, and a spoiler to filter air drag on the highway.

With an increasing number of innovations, there are more choices for you to choose from. Best sites to provide you with reviews related to motorcycle helmets include:

- Carbibles.com

- Bikebandit.com

- Revzilla.com

Inflatable mattresses

One of the most popular markets that have been solid for a long time. An inflatable mattress is the best choice for a regular bed. One can use it for college dorms, camping or guests. There is a good market for these, and it just keeps getting more popular with more choices than ever. Use the sites below to read reviews for inflatable mattresses.

- Best.offers.com

- Bestmattress.reviews

- Bestreviews.com

Pet Supplies

Many families own at least one pet. Others own more than one pet. The trend has been growing daily, and that has increased the demand for pet supplies.

When you consider all different types of pets kept by people, you will realize that the supply these animals need is large. That shows how this is a lucrative niche that will continue to grow. Some of the sites dedicated to reviewing pet supplies include:

- Nymag.com/strategist

- Gooddoginabox.com

- Rsreview.com

Pillows

Low ticket vs. high ticket Affiliate Marketing

Most of the commission offered by companies is low because their products are priced low. A commission of 40% or less is common. For instance, you can market a book for $50 and only receive a $15 commission, or a video course that sells for $300, and receive a commission of only $80. They will scarcely pay on the back-end. In fact, most companies are greedy and lazy to offer a percentage of the extra money they generate from the customers you sent them. This explains why some of the successful online affiliate marketers give up. Without the back-end commissions, it's hard for them to make a decent profit to promote low priced products.

Think about it this way, would you prefer to sell 1,000 products each month getting paid a commission of $10 per product or sell ten products that pay $1,000 commission each? Let's imagine that your goal is to raise $10, 000 per month.

Although both offer you $10,000 each month, one is more comfortable than the other.

High-ticket marketing

Realizing the difference between traditional affiliate marketing and high-ticket affiliate marketing can rapidly increase your income. One of the drawbacks of traditional affiliate marketing is that one is only paid on front-end sales. The front-end sales are the low-ticket items.

For instance, if you refer a customer and they purchased a $100 product, depending on the site that you have sent them to, your commission will range between 2-50%. In some rare cases, certain programs will provide you with on front-end sales.

Once you dive in online marketing, you will realize that it costs money to generate traffic to your pages. You will need to pay money before you can advertise. Making low-ticket commissions isn't going to be better for you unless you sell huge volumes.

Adding high-ticket products to your portfolio can boost your commissions. For instance, if you can refer your customers to a particular product that costs $2, 000 and you receive 50% commission, then you will be paid $1,000 if the customer buys the product.

Higher commissions imply that you don't need as many sales to make a reliable income from your business each month.

How does it work?

Few people go for the high-ticket products right away. In most cases, they want to test a free product to see if they like the quality or not.

For you to access high-ticket affiliate commissions, you must look for companies that bind the customer to you using a lifelong cookie. In other words, they will share the commissions with you on all the future sales from customers they referred.

When you have multiple avenues with progressively high prices and benefits, it is usually called a Tiered Product Mix.

So why do you need a Tiered Product Mix

Take the example of Apple. The people who purchased the iPod when it was released saw the need to change their phones to an iPhone. They could even choose to shift from a PC to a Mac. One reason is that they had the opportunity to test a lower ticker item from Apple and enjoyed the quality. Now it is not a big problem for them to come back and look out what other product Apple has in the market. The fact that the products work smoothly with each other is an added advantage for them to continue to buy from the same company.

This is a way of building a long-term relationship with a customer. Something that you can find with high-ticket affiliate marketing.

For one to make use of high-ticket affiliate marketing programs, you will need to pay for a membership fee or a licensing agreement with a vendor. In return, they offer you access to a high-ticket commission.

Chapter 3: Steps to Become an Affiliate Marketer

Coming up with the product idea

Most people find it hard to develop a product idea. But that is not the case. Ideas are easy to create. In fact, your product idea doesn't have to be super original or arise from the pure genius of your brain. That is very hard. If you want to make money with affiliate marketing, you don't need to be romantically attached to your idea.

But simply try to identify products and services that are already out there. Try to figure out how you can improve upon these products, by delivering something that will solve problems by using those products. Of course, you can decide to select a product that you're interested or involved in.

Assume that you are a stay-at-home Dad, for a second. Maybe you plan to develop a product that simplifies household chores. For instance, you can search for a vacuum robot to get some tips.

With a simple google search, you will find individual reviews. If you read individual reviews, it is easy for you to tell what is bad about these robots and what you can improve.

Another method that you can apply to research is by using the Buzzsumo tool; this tool will allow you to see what is popular based on social shares. Whether you start to build Sandcastles, you will be able to see the most recent content instantly.

Validate your idea

The next step once you have a product idea is to validate your idea. Instead of creating a series of videos that no one is going to purchase, it is important to validate your idea. Well, how can you validate your idea?

The answer is simple. You can ask people to pay you for it. Now the next question that you will ask yourself is how do you find these people. Easy. Select a URL related to your product idea and enter it into a tool called Topsy.

Topsy will reveal to you a list of all the people who tweeted that particular link. Next, you can tell these people more about your idea by hitting the reply button. Remember to ask them whether or not they would purchase your idea. Not just whether they like it. Anyone can say they love something as a way to be nice. But if they reply with a yes, you should follow them up with a request to buy.

Someone saying that they will spend money isn't the same as spending it. When people are interested in your product, offer them a chance to purchase. You can easily integrate PayPal and let them know that you are going to create it once you receive a specific number of orders.

Once you pass your threshold and ensure that people really want it, you can now start to create your product.

Building the product

There are a lot of steps to follow when you want to create a product. It is easy to create a digital product since it will only require time and some financial investment, but it can't be more than a service fee or a one-time price for software.

Once you create a product and deliver it your original buyers, that will be the time for you to open up your affiliate network.

Starting your first affiliate website

Building your affiliate website is a great way to make money online. It is good because it feels good to make money while building a resource that people will actually get value from. If you are yet to explore it, building an affiliate marketing website is a genuine business model that can generate thousands of dollars per month in affiliate commissions.

Selecting your niche

In this section, you'll learn about building your first affiliate website. When it comes to building an affiliate website, the first thing that you should think about is not related to hosting, or domain names, or even website software.

The first thing to decide is what your website is going to feature. Since your goal is to earn money using affiliate marketing, you need to be careful about this decision.

Narrow in the niche

Narrowing down your niche means that you concentrate most of your energy serving a small group of people. This makes everything easy for you to:

1. Find people.

2. Realize their pain points.

3. Deliver it to them in a way that makes them feel like you understand them.

Since you are not trying to deliver something to a large group with mixed interests and pain points, you can choose to speak to your niche in a way that sounds creepy because you will be getting right inside their head.

Niches within niches

Let's assume your target audience is the fitness niche. That is a bit broad. In fact, if you ask anyone, they will tell you that they want to be fit. It is difficult to build a site that targets everyone because how will you get people attracted to it without having to spend a bucket load of money.

The most important thing to note is that there are niches within niches and it is easy and cheaper to focus on these than a broader niche.

For example, the fitness niche can further be divided into:

1. Healthy eating

2. Cardio

3. Yoga

4. Pilates

5. Exercise

6. Weight loss

That will break up the fitness niche into a targeted segment. Niches within niches.

We can break that down further. For example, "Cardio."

You have many different types of cardio.

1. Rowing

2. Cycling

3. Swimming

4. Boxing

5. Circuit training

6. Long distance running

7. Rope-jumping

This will break down the fitness niche into a specific segment.

But don't go too deep.

If you can concentrate on a specific niche that can help you reach out to your specific audience.

For instance, if you create a site around the niche of Rowing for Fitness. There is a chance for you to narrow that into Rowing for Weight-loss that can offer you some lateral movement to topics such as diet.

But make sure that you don't go too deep with your niche selection.

Ensure that it has a future affiliate chance

You want to ensure that the niche you choose has lots of affiliate opportunities. Think about these people and at least 4 or 5 types of products that they may want to buy; it might be right if you can consider other niches too.

If you want to verify that there are existing affiliate opportunities for you to register some affiliate networks, look for specific products that you can check for that niche and confirm that you get paid for recommending online.

There is no pain to do the following step, and it will take just less than an hour in most cases to receive confirmation about whether you have something to promote or not.

It is a bit cheap to spend 1-hour to look for products to promote as opposed to spending hundreds of hours to create a site and then you lack options to promote.

Step by step to building your own website

Once you have chosen your niche. You are now ready for the next step to build your first website.

Below are some of the things that you need to build your website.

- A web host
- A content plan
- A web host
- A domain name
- A website content management software.

Easy. Right? Only four things!

Don't be worried about this stuff. Nowadays, with a click of a button, you will install all the moving parts — no need to hire a coder or programmer to do it for you.

Domain name

Now that you have chosen your niche, it should be easy for you to tell me what you want to call your website. If you are yet to decide, spend some time to research and identify your niche. A website domain is generally an easy way for someone to refer their web browser to your site.

Instead of typing all the IP address, a website domain simplifies everything. You only need to remember the name. Another way for you to think about it is like the address for your house. A space that you rent on a server. In other words, your website is the house.

What about Content Management Software?

Traditionally, anyone who wanted to build a website, they had to learn how to program HTML. HTML is a special language that reveals to the browser what a website looks like.

That is where Content Management Software comes into play or CMS for short. So CMS is a software that performs the HTML coding. It will store all the articles that you write in a database.

When a person visits a page on your website, the CMS will fetch the title of the page and show it to the visitor.

The best CMS software is the WordPress. Virtually, 54% of the whole internet runs on WordPress with the remaining percent made up of custom-made sites and smaller CMS systems. It is advised to go with the WordPress website because it is easy to get a specialist in WordPress. The reason is that WordPress is a popular platform.

Choosing your domain name provider and web host

Selecting the best domain name can be hard for someone who is starting out with affiliate marketing. Let's assume that you have chosen a niche for your affiliate marketing website, so you need to know already what your site is going to feature. Now it is the time to pick a domain name that you like and one that is available. This can be a little difficult, but great domain names can still be hard.

Bluehost is an example of a website host that has been in existence for the past 20 years. They host over 2 million websites. They have competitive prices. Also, they have their own servers and facilities located in Utah, USA. With just a click of a button, you can install everything.

When it comes to prices, they offer affordable charges. For example, one can choose a hosting plan that is less than USD 50 a year.

Creating a content plan

To build your content plan, you first require to understand and make use of a few concepts which will allow you to organize the parts of your content.

Let's discuss something about visitor funnels.

A funnel, in marketing terms, is a means of choosing a large number of visitors and subjecting them through various steps to reduce the number to only those that are going to follow the action that you want.

Don't forget that the end goal of your affiliate website is to generate money by helping and referring people to services and products and get paid for it.

A visitor funnel will provide you with direct traffic, certify something and sell them something.

The intention of the visitor

The intention of the visitors is an important factor that you need to work hard to learn. This will help you choose the main content pieces that you need to build.

Intent describes what the visitor's desires, needs and wants at different stages of the buying journey. But not all visitors are the same. People may be at various stages of their journey in your specific niche when they visit your website.

The intention of each group of people at various stages is different although they may be related to the niche. This is a primary concept that you need to understand when building your content plan because if you recognize the intention of your visitor, you are at a better stage to know the type of content that you must create.

Adding a funnel

If you can brainstorm article ideas for your visitor intent, the next thing to do is to build the funnel. As mentioned previously, a funnel will take a motivated person and place them on a journey to buy. A funnel also works best when you are aware of the intention of the visitor so that you can match the intent with the correct offer.

This is all presenting them with the right offer at the right time. To achieve that, you will want to build multiple funnels. One per visitor intent that you have selected.

The first thing that should come to the top is to get people to your site. That is right at the top of your funnel. The next thing is to get those people onto your mailing list by giving them something that they can't resist.

Funnel bait

This is the tool that you will use to get people into your funnel; it can be in the form of a PDF guide, a spreadsheet, checklist, and some free software. Or something that is easy to put together that you will want at that visitor intent stage. The more desirable the bait is; the more people will come for your funnel.

Tips to consider when creating content for your affiliate website

There are specific contents that are written to market an affiliate product in a way that your website visitors can understand and relate to generate a conversion, affiliate links, and sales. You must have come across these types of content while you read through websites, blogs, and other affiliate websites. Well, but how effective are the following sites?

This section shares with you everything that you must know when you want to market your affiliate product. Let's get started right away.

1. Write the truth

The biggest mistake that you can make in affiliate marketing is to write about a product that you have never tested before, or have no personal experience. Instead of making this mistake, focus on the truth, what you know is true about the product.

And here is the reason why. The visitors to your website trust you and the opinion you say about a product that you share with them. When you suggest a product, your readers will jump on it right away.

So, when you create a review, make sure that you write an honest review. Then share it with your visitors. Let them not think like you want to make money from it. That is why it is good if you can tell them reasons why they should buy the product and the reasons why they should not buy the product. You must avoid getting biased.

When you have this in mind, you will never find yourself pitching for products that you have never used or don't like. Your audience will be able to realize, and you'll lose readers and credibility.

To take it a step further, mention to your readers exactly about what you loved about a specific product, and go an extra step to point out how it benefited you, improve your life, or it gave you something special that will make them take an interest in.

2. Stay Relevant

With affiliate marketing content, the reader is the center of focus, and it should remain like this forever. So for your affiliate marketing to be successful, make sure that you keep your reader at the center of it by checking that your article passes the relevancy score. Don't be biased. While writing, put yourself in the shoes of your readers. What is that they will be thinking? What is it that they want and how much are they ready to invest in it?

Even more, you should be thinking about why they want it and what they'll gain from using it.

These things can have a long-term impact on the value of your affiliate marketing content, and can further show that you care about the readers and you are ready to step into their shoes.

3. Easy to read content

When you create content that is easy to read and scan, it adds a great impression, especially to your readers. No need to scare them with lengthy, uninterrupted text. When you craft your content for affiliate marketing, make sure that you have a readable content. According to a study by Jakob Nielsen, only 20% of the text is read on average. This means that most people don't read but simply scan a page.

People want to find what they are looking for without reading through the entire content. So it is good to customize your posts to make it easy for readers to scan. Below are some great ways that you can make your readers enjoy to read your content.

1. Use subheadings.

2. Make short paragraphs.

3. Use a high-quality picture.

4. Include videos.

5. Apply readable fonts.

6. Make use of lists.

7. Highlight crucial points.

4. Be natural when you create your story

If you are writing a review about an affiliate product that you want to promote, write it in a way that is friendly to your blog readers. It should not appear like a direct product marketing as it will affect the other side which will cut down your total sales.

One rule that you should remember in marketing is that if your audience doesn't love it, then they won't purchase it. So whenever you are crafting an affiliate marketing content, keep that in mind. Make sure that you include some descriptions and recommendations about a specific product.

Testimonials from other users will add more value to your writing.

This will ensure that your content remains fresh and allows you to build a quality readership and trust over the product described in your blog post.

Such actions rapidly boost your total sales because your blog content allows you to create a relationship with your readers from promotions.

5. Concentrate on products that customers enjoy

Your customers should be the mainstream of your affiliate marketing. If you don't focus on goods, products, and services that they love, you are already missing the mark. Although we have said it is important to feature only products that you love, it is still important to remember that your preferences and readers won't just appear easily.

When that happens, it is important to consider the preference of your customers because they are the ones who will benefit from affiliate marketing.

When you have this in mind, you must work hard so that you can provide things that will benefit your customers and readers. And they shall thank you for it. Don't forget that this will make you succeed as an affiliate marketer.

6. Use different resources

The affiliate business promotes usage of products in real time life, and thus trust is an important thing. Let your content be fresh every time. No one will buy your product via Twitter or Facebook promotion or visit your blog and click a banner to proceed with the purchase.

Most will want to find out what they require about a product and whether the product fulfills their needs. It can be anything or any resource such as a social mention, brand mention over flyers, emails, etc. You must try to use every kind of platform to market your product naturally in a way that readers will improve your business.

Use different marketing strategies to generate traffic from various sources that will allow you to widen the market and increase your sales.

Guide to crafting content on your affiliate website that will rank well

Now that you have learned the tips on how you can build your website. We provide you with an additional guide that you can use to ensure that your content ranks well. Every online marketer knows that content is key. It is the best way to advertise a brand and an effective marketing tool. It does a wide variety of functions that may not be related to marketing itself, but the result is great.

Content marketing is one of the easiest and cheapest tools that takes marketing to a new dimension. But for you to make it work, it is good to remember that the content should have to be linked to similar websites and resources. That is affiliate marketing, and it will help your brand discover an online niche and the right audience for marketing services or goods.

Content and Affiliate Marketing

How does content affect affiliate marketing? Well, consider the case where you visit a given website to read a couple of articles. Then you find some interesting title and begin to read the post. You come across links that redirect you to other sites, and you click these links because the content is incredible and you expect to find something even interesting. That is how content works. You make use of another content platform to derive attention of their audience to your website, product or service.

The practical value of a post

The biggest question is how a post can catch the attention of an audience. Some of the challenges that you will face while you start to create your content include, you don't have a solid knowledge of your audience. Or the audience may not be interested in what you provide them.

As a result, you need to select a successful affiliate marketing website to post your articles. Remember that you share a similar audience. Let's find out what makes people want to click on articles that catch their attention.

First, as an affiliate marketer, you must ensure that the post you create has practical value for the readers. In other words, your readers should learn ideas that will help them solve problems or even improve the quality of their work and life.

How can data-driven posts increase traffic

One thing that you must consider is that your post should contain enough data and statistics. People enjoy to check on stats, and they will perhaps look for an article that will promise them results. Obviously, the stats that you select should be associated with the audience, and the audience should show interest in that particular data. That is the only way you can succeed to direct traffic to your website through affiliate marketing.

Strategies to copywriting

To craft an amazing post, stats isn't enough for readers; you need to make sure that you write it in clear words that will assist you to reach out to your specific audience. Words should be your major weapon, and you must know how to apply the power of copywriting.

Different approaches will assist you to create a perfect content.

-Storytelling

-The right application of CTA

-AIDA (Attention, Interest, Desire, and Action).

When you apply these strategies to your writing, you'll be able to have the correct copy.

The structure of a great affiliate post

Remember that how your post appears is important to the reader. It is a known fact that everyone prefers to read a post that is well-organized and has a clear introduction, main body, and conclusion.

All the paragraphs and sentences must be short. Just remember that each paragraph should present an idea or message. You can move on and divide the main body as much as you want, but remember to link up the paragraphs and respect the hierarchy of the post.

To create the right structure of a post, make sure that you apply special marks and symbols that will assist you to change the readability. But before you publish your post, it is important to proofread symbols chart to verify that you don't miss any detail that is important.

Apply SEO in the content creation process

It is not just enough to publish an article on a given affiliate website, and you must do something on the SEO so that you can drive traffic to your post. Below we provide you a quick guide of some of the things that you can implement so that you improve the chances of your content recognized by search engines.

- **Pick the correct keywords**

The keywords have to be relevant to the topic of your article. Don't stick to one type of keyword but try to have different kinds of keywords. However, don't overuse keywords because Google will penalize you for keyword stuffing.

- **Define the length of your post**

The best length of an article should be 2,000 words.

- **Mobile optimization**

Confirm whether your content looks attractive in a mobile device. Additionally, make sure that the place where you want to post your article is perfect for mobile phones.

- **On-page optimization**

Next, add keywords to the metatags. The description, title, h1, and alt texts should feature keywords so that your post ranks better.

- **In-bound links**

Insert a link into a reliable source to boost the ranking of your article.

Content types to boost your affiliate website

As said before, to drive traffic and involve your audience, content is a must in affiliate website. But not all content is crafted equally. If you focus so much on blog posts, you may end up limiting the effectiveness of your website.

Conversely, if you create the right content for your audience, it can positively affect your sales and raise your business. With a different type of content for your site, you can attain new heights and deliver more to your target audience.

This section highlights for you the major types of content that you should have on your affiliate website. This includes how you can create each content and make use of it.

1. The "How to guides."

These particular guides assist a reader in seeing how they can carry out a particular task. They are mostly used by affiliate marketers to offer instant value to readers. Additionally, since they are a bit long in length, it improves the search engine rank.

In case you don't know how to create the how-to guide, no worries. There are a few tips to get you started. These tips help you create a comprehensive and useful guide for your audience.

- **Know what to include.** While you do your research, keep a list of the types of content that other how-to guides create, and make some notes of what is missing. Next, combine the list when you start to create your how-to guide.

- Use a structure that is easy to follow. Make sure that you break each structure into smaller chunks. You can choose to include an outline to guide your readers where they should go.

The most important thing is that your how-to guides must keep your readers' needs in mind at all times. The best way to do is to put yourself in the shoes of your reader and think about some of the questions and concerns that they may have. This way you will be able to include the answers to your guide.

2. Product reviews

Perhaps you spend most of the time marketing products. For that reason, product reviews can be an excellent addition to your content marketing program. Product reviews generate value to your readers while allowing you to include natural affiliate links to the products that you trust. But make sure that the products are customized to fulfill the needs of your customers. Below are two extra tips that you must consider.

- Use a product before you review it. Although this is not possible, using a product gives you a chance to learn everything about a product so that you can cover every aspect when you write a review.

- Make use of an easy to understand system. For instance, rate your products using a five-star or a scale of 1-10. Another option is the report card system which includes A-F letter grades. Just remember that product reviews are very popular. You'll have to be different from your competitors to stand a chance in the market. The most important way of doing this is to deliver in-depth and actionable content.

3. Video tutorials

In one way, video tutorials are associated with how-to guides. But these improve the teaching process by applying an interactive approach. Additionally, they can assist you to address a wider audience. With online video viewing on the rise, you can't miss taking part.

To start, you must have a camera and a microphone, and a broadcasting platform. However, if you would like to take your video tutorials to the next level, below are two tips that can keep you going.

- **Understand the needs of your audience beforehand.** Similar to the how-to guides, it is not sufficient to demonstrate to your website visitors how to carry out a given task. But be sure to identify the kind of problems that your audience faces and address them specifically.

- **Offer opportunities for viewer interaction.** This can include hosting live video tutorials and interacting with your viewers. There are many platforms such as Facebook, YouTube, and Instagram.

4. Email newsletters

An email newsletter is a content that you sent out to your subscribers. It can include anything that you may decide to write. For marketers, newsletters are a brilliant way because they permit you to contact subscribers outside your website. Their flexible structure will also make it possible to become creative in the content that you deliver. But you should keep the following in mind.

- **Encourage reader interaction.** For instance, ask questions or share links to your latest blog posts.

- **Incorporate a strong call to action.** This is crucial for all types of content. Since you deliver newsletters on a different platform, your CTAs should support readers to scan through your site or social media profile.

Essentially, you should learn to target your readers while building the content. If you can consider your audience, you will increase the odds of interaction.

Chapter 4: Choosing an Affiliate Program

Which affiliate Path to take?

Before affiliates earn referral revenue, they need to have an active audience to share third-party offers with. An offer is like an agreement from a brand to help pay an affiliate commission for referring a business. Affiliates get commission when a person they referred to an advertiser buys their product or accomplishes an agreed action such as signing up for the niche's email list. This is also called referral marketing, and it's the basic model that affiliate earn revenue.

Creating an email list, extending your social media following, and attracting website visitors is a vital step to success in affiliate marketing. Without an active audience, affiliates would require to pay for media every time they want to market an offer. That leaves them with narrow opportunities that won't pay when the attention of the buyer is competitive to earn. It's similar to purchasing a new cup every time you need to drink water. This is not the best solution, and it is better to grow an audience of your own.

However, building an online presence is only part of the journey to establishing a successful affiliate marketing business. After all the effort you put in, time, and financial investment of building an active audience, it is important for affiliates to ensure that they focus most on delivering high-quality experiences.

Working with affiliate marketing companies

Affiliate companies offer the best results because they have an established cost-per-acquisition model. Affiliates are registered to market a product or service, and if an affiliate creates a sale, then they get a commission. This means that the company pays out only when a sale has already been secured.

Partnering with affiliate marketing companies has many benefits. The CPA model means that they provide a low-risk strategy that can deliver better results. It is a performance driven method that only rewards affiliate members who convert sales. Advertisers don't pay-out unless the campaign is determined successful. This also implies that affiliate marketing companies don't receive any payment unless the campaign yields positive results.

The way this model is built encourages high performance. It is the interest of the affiliate marketing company to get the best results for their advertisers. If they don't, they don't receive any payment either. As a result, the best affiliate marketing companies will grill publishers to ensure an effective partnership with quality affiliates.

Another advantage of affiliate marketing companies is that they deal with all types of management. It is like turning on a channel on autopilot so that you can deal with other areas. They will handle the day-to-day programs and keep you updated with regular reports. You can then manage to work on other marketing projects, confident that your affiliate channel is yielding revenue in the background. And in case you need to get a quick response, your affiliate manager is waiting at the other end with all the information you need.

Tips for choosing the best Affiliate Programs

You may have read or heard someone say that affiliate marketing is one the best ways to make money online without selling your products. Well, but if you have done some research, you must come to realize how difficult it is when you want to choose the right affiliate program for your site. Getting this step right is important because even if you have a lot of visitors coming to your site, your conversion rates may be low especially when they aren't attracted to what you have to provide them. To ensure that you get the best from your traffic, here are some tips for you to use when looking for the best affiliate programs in your niche.

1. Pick an affiliate program that you can honestly recommend

Most affiliate marketers tell new beginners to use this tip because it works. If you are using a specific product which you are sure it works so well, then it would be simple to come up with an excellent review that would force your visitors to purchase it. Online users want a product that they can relate with. Uploading your pictures while using the product gives them the confidence and feel for what the product would be like in their hands.

2. Research the biggest affiliate networks

This tip would not work for everyone. However, it is still possible to find products to sell in your blog even when you haven't tried them before. In most cases, manufacturers and brand teams work together with affiliate networks rather than setting up their own affiliate program. This is because thousands of affiliates are already registered to following networks. It is easy to find any product you think of. Just take time to do a deep research about the product before you can recommend it on your site.

3. Find out the rates of commission

There could be cases where you can find a high-quality product that is perfect to sell on your site for a low commission rate. This is a critical factor when selecting an affiliate program. Even when your site receives a lot of traffic, you may not generate good money if you earn a very low commission rate for the sales you make. But if you can research well, you'll find affiliate networks that are known for high commission rates. These sites will give you a chance to earn a substantial amount for your sales.

4. Evaluate the support system

The last thing that you don't want is to work with an affiliate network that doesn't have an effective communication system. When something goes wrong, especially with regards to payment, you want their support team to respond to all the questions.

Huge support is needed for any product, and that is not different when looking out for the best affiliate partners. Without this, you will have the worst experience when you market products and report progress on sales. Even worse, this can affect your customers and the people you recommend the product to.

Most affiliate programs connect you with an affiliate manager. This is a person whom you can communicate directly when something goes wrong or when you have a question that you want to be addressed.

The affiliate manager can as well provide you with general tips that will be helpful in affiliate marketing. So you must be confident to work with your affiliate manager.

5. Program Competitors

If you're already successful on a given affiliate program, take time to review some of the brand's competitor to find out whether they have affiliate programs to join. Giving your audience additional products in the same category or even from direct competitors will increase the chances for conversion. Although your blog deals with different products, most of your customers may be more inclined to purchase from a given category of featured items.

6. Preferred by your audience

Whatever affiliate programs you choose to promote, it must be something that your audience desires. The first thing is to understand exactly who your target audience is. There are different ways of doing this, but it should start by building a customer profile. Be specific and make the person you are selling to as real as possible. If you have a customer base in place, use this define who is buying your current products. Once you have defined your target audience, perform some research. If you want the affiliate marketing programs you select to sell well, make sure that you commit time.

7. Upsells

Upsells offer an additional method to increase commission. Once the consumer has bought the original product, he is provided different packages that are present at the time of purchase. This method is called upselling. For affiliate, if the buyer takes advantage of the following offers, the rate of commission increases.

For instance, a consumer may click on a laptop, and at checkout, he or she is offered a new deal that includes a remote mouse and laptop case. In case this person picks the offer, they will receive a commission on the extra products.

8. Vendor reputation

Merchants also start their businesses at a certain point, but it is better to work with long experienced vendors who have a good reputation and high traffic. Do your research and ensure they tick all the boxes above. Don't be discouraged by new vendors if they are providing an excellent product and a good commission rate.

A strong affiliate marketing networks offer conversion metrics, which will give you the chance to see merchants convert their visitors to sales well. New vendors may not have any metrics to report, so this could be a reason to wait before you can commit to them.

When you select a product, how much you want to earn is important, but you will realize that you are very successful with the programs that you are genuinely passionate about. When you sell something that you are interested in, your customers can tell it right away. This can be the best choice to make.

9. Recurring commissions

Recurring commissions are a great way for an affiliate to increase their income. Examples of recurring services include hosting, VPN, and autoresponders. If a person registers for a monthly cycle and they continue to use the service, he or she receives a specific payment for every month.

10. High ticket vs. high volume

A high-ticket item is one that has a high selling price. A high-ticket item will also have more value and can last for a longer time. In the gem of affiliate marketing, you focus mostly on the sale price. That is the same reason that you must focus on products that generate high value.

High ticket items sell at a high cost. This means the amount of commission is high. The best high-ticket products are the ones which you work directly with the manufacturer.

The reason why super affiliates like high ticket items is because it is easy to convert 100 prospects on a $1000 product than it is to convert 10, 000 people, to buy a $10 product, both of which will generate $100k in revenue.

There are a few things to consider before you decide to market high ticket items. First, if you are good at spotting trends and searching for the next big product, then there is a high chance to make millions by selling low ticket items before others realize.

Next, is the level of competition. If everybody is promoting high ticket items and no one is taking time to market low-ticket items, then you can use that chance to make a good income from low-ticket items.

11. Trust

Whether you are working with a right brand or an affiliate network, trust is the most critical factor. Honesty must be present about the clicks and conversion data.

Also, you must trust that the affiliate networks will maintain their links. You may have to do some trial and error before you can select the best affiliate network.

12. User friendliness and experience

When searching for the best affiliate program, you also want to consider the software that they use to support the affiliate dashboard. Are the dashboards easy to find ads and look for a comprehensive report?

The best Affiliate networks

Well, this is the best part that probably you have been waiting for, as a new beginner you will want to know which are the best affiliate programs.

1. Amazon associates

They are one of the largest eCommerce company across the world. The success of Amazon mainly comes from hundreds of thousands of associates that have worked tirelessly to create content to market on their site.

The best thing when you collaborate with Amazon, it provides you with a long list of physical products and informational products such as ebooks.

If you have a website, you may have a lot of high-quality products to market on your site. Amazon gives you the best deal because they adjust the commission percentage for some products.

Amazon is one of the best affiliate programs that one can sign up for. But experienced affiliate marketers have signed up for alternatives and searched for smaller networks to work with. You must learn to diversify your business.

2. eBay

Many people know about eBay as an online E-commerce company. However, only a few people know that they also have an affiliate network program. The eBay Partner Network has been in existence for a long time, and it has been tested with thousands of content creators.

Similar to Amazon, eBay has different kinds of physical products in many categories. Some of these products have a higher conversion rate because of their recognizable brand.

For example, you can generate between 50% and 70% of the auction fees generated on the sales and the duration of the cookie changes from 24hours for Buy it Now products and ten days for the products that are listed for auction.

Don't forget that eBay does not sell the products, but individuals list the products on the website for sale. eBay only receives a specific fee from the sale, and the commission depends on the amount instead of the price of the product.

3. ClickBank

ClickBank is a pioneer of info products, and it has been running the business since 1998. They have a lot of products that they offer to affiliates. In other words, it is easy for you to get a chance to market an info product on your website.

The company features a simple website that is easy to use, and you can as well search and filter products. If you are a content creator, you can decide to build an info product of your own and sell on ClickBank. Other affiliates can then promote it for you.

4. Shareasale

ShareASale is another large affiliate network. The platform has about 4,000 merchants out of which One thousand are exclusive to them. ShareASale publishes a large amount of data on every offer they run. Some of their offers include:

- Reversal rates

- Earnings per Click

- Average Sale Amount

- Average Commission

Advantages of ShareASale

- It is a large partner network. They have more than 4, 000 merchants.

- It is easy to compare offers. When you select from the various offers, ShareASale simplifies the process so that you can choose the best ones based on the metrics.

- A quick payment Cycle.

5. Maxbounty

This is a new player in the affiliate world. The company was established in 2004 in Ottawa, Canada. It is considered as the only affiliate network designed for affiliates. It has a Cost Per Action plan that focuses on ad banners. The company operates in the business niche and boasts of over,1500 active campaigns.

The company focuses only on digital products. This involves sending out one's email. They have Pay-Per-Call campaigns for someone to select.

The average rate of commission depends on the type of campaign.

6. CJ Affiliate

CJ Affiliate is one of the biggest affiliate platforms online. If you have worked in the affiliate marketing platform for a specific period, you may have come across them.

Most retailers have registered their affiliate programs on CJ Affiliate. The site offers different ad sizes for affiliates. With many different types of advertisers on CJ Affiliate platform, it is easy to make a comparison and segment various offers.

7. Affiliate Window –(AWIN)

This network claims to have worked with over 13, 000 active advertisers and 100, 000 publishers. The network is active in more than 11 countries.

Established in 2000, the company has become popular in the UK and across the world. Currently, it has over 1,600 brands across 77 sectors in 11 territories around the world. AWIN has a simple, and friendly dashboard to help affiliates market their campaigns.

8. VigLink

This network is different from other affiliate programs. The network was created mainly for bloggers. In this network, affiliates don't choose the merchants to work with, but the company has a dynamic link that changes to work with verified merchants that offer the best conversion rates.

In other words, VigLink acts as a middleman between the publisher and merchants. The company works with all types of advertisers, but it doesn't classify them based on what's popular.

VigLink only concentrates on selling physical products, but it also works with some digital services and products.

Who can use VigLink

This is a third-party platform that acts as a backdoor for affiliates who have been removed or suspended from working with a specific affiliate program like Amazon. While you can choose individual merchants, VigLink can work automatically by scanning published content and generating dynamic affiliate links.

Pros of using Viglink

- Work across different social networks.

- The best choice if you are banned from using Amazon and other affiliate programs.

- It can be set dynamically to update links to optimize income.

- It is best for bloggers who are searching for a hands-off affiliate network.

Cons of VigLink

- You must get approved by every merchant separately.

- The automatic link creation has to be fine-tuned.

- A huge gap in the payouts between merchants.

- Payment is only once a month

9. JVZoo

This network with digital products, mainly e-commerce, internet marketing, and online courses. JVZoo is a good competitor for ClickBank and other affiliate networks.

Types of Products

JVZoo mainly deals with online courses. Additionally, it created a leadership role in marketing product releases, which take place every day.

Average rate commission

The rate of commission varies based on the product, but most of them offer 50 percent of higher returns.

Who can use it?

The company allows affiliates to create landing pages on their websites. This means it the best platform for professional marketers who want to publish information about product offers. But you don't need to own a website to use JVZoo, but you may only need to learn how to drive traffic to a landing page to generate commission.

The advantage of JVZoo is that it gives permission to experienced marketers to access product releases and online courses. This is not the best platform for that person who wants to make cash by allowing users to click through various physical products.

10. AdCombo

This is a CPA Marketing Network that has its own in-house technology to make it possible for one to customize advertising campaigns to satisfy the needs of a targeted audience across the world. They purpose to hit their target audience in facilitating a lucrative strategic partnership between advertisers and publishers to monetize their traffic.

11. ReviMedia

This is an online lead generation network that is focused on owned and campaigns related to insurance, financial verticals, and home services. Additionally, the company has their proprietary lead management platform that provides a better scoring of each insight based on the demographic information. The company is highly flexible to run campaigns with a wide variety of integrations. They boast on their transparency with clients as well as a flexible term of payment. The company also grants advertising partners you access to an extensive direct publisher network of over 2, 000 publishers.

Check your niche on AdWords

If you are selling products, services or ideas, then Google ad-words may be of great help to you. In the niche industry, selling a service or a product is not a bad thing as long as you market it well. Good marketing will attract potential consumers to buy your product or idea.

Ideas are similar to niches because they focus on a specific mindset

The steps to a niche

1. Choose your customer

The niche markets require a comprehensive computation. These are areas which need to a detail research.

2. Customer segments are the main segments

The basic segmentation is not enough; you must consider the customer segments.

3. Fill the gaps left by others

By fulfilling the requirements of the customer in a specific niche may not be enough. You must try to fix the little differences in your service. Build a strong, and unique selling proposition.

4. In case space is small, it is a must that there will be people pushing and shoving it.

The opposite belief is that only a large general market is competitive. If you are searching for the floor space, then you must ensure that you position the service before anything else.

5. Take advantage of Google Ad-words

Ad-words are useful in this situation. Ad-words are keywords specific, and it will provide one with the power to reach out to a specific audience such as social media.

6. Selecting AdWords

By choosing Adwords to get into the niche markets, it means that you must create the best focus of your intended product.

Steps to determine whether your niche ideas are profitable

When you have a list of your niche ideas, it is better to decide whether your niche ideas are valuable or not. It is good if you can decide whether or not you can get your target audience online. So let's see how you can find out whether your niche profitable or not.

1. Google search volume for your niche idea

When you can find out the number of people looking for your niche idea and associated keywords on Google is the first step. They are the largest search engine in the world where most of the traffic is going to originate from.

While keyword research is not a complete picture, just a small part of the more significant process, it reveals instant demand. So you can start here before you dig deeper by doing this.

Use a google keyword planner: Free Version

When you use a Google Keyword Planner tool, the first step is to sign up for an account and log in if you have one. No need to pay for anything or add a credit. Once you finish, you click on the "Get search volume data and trends."

Then simply type your niche idea or keywords.

Before you can make a search, choose your locations or whichever country you'd like to target. Still, there is the option to search all locations on your home country. This will also work fine too. Remember. You are simply looking for an idea if something is popular or not, don't get caught up in what you select.

2. Search for trends in Google

A quick look on Google Trends to make sure that it is not a dying trend is a great idea. It is advised to concentrate on evergreen niches than trends that come and disappear.

Just type your keyword or niche idea in the search bar and determine whether it's rising or at least a stable niche.

Though it's worth not to keep in mind that simply because something isn't as popular as it once was doesn't imply it's no longer profitable. Certain things have a lot of interest because they are all over the media or go viral.

Others get spikes at different times of the years due to being seasonal. Then that particular interest disappears.

It doesn't imply that they aren't profitable, but it's important to consider why the trend is moving downward or spiked before you try to make money from the niche.

But remember to list down what you found out in your Word document or notepad. If you are using a Word, then you can take screenshots for future reference.

3. Do you have products on sale?

The best niches are the ones with both digital products and one that is present for sale. Although a good number of niches will only be one or the other and that isn't a problem as long as there's a great selection of products and a demand for them.

For instance, internet marketing is one of the most profitable niches present, but it's is only digital products on sale. So it is good to check on the affiliate networks whether there are already products on sale and they are selling well. There's no particular volume or number you should be looking for.

You simply want a proof to see that some people buy in that niche and high volumes.

4. Determine the level of competitiveness of your niche keyword phrases

You will also need to analyze how competitive each keyword phrase is, you must evaluate the relative difficulty of ranking every niche keyword. However, relative competition isn't enough to conduct this kind of analysis.

Successful keyword targeting calls for constant monitoring and tweaking. You have invested a lot of money and time into choosing the best niche keyword opportunities. Now you can move on to accrue investment by constantly monitoring how the same keywords perform on your site and by particular business goals. It's important for you to remember that simply because a keyword tool returns a keyword doesn't imply that you will manage to rank for it or that the traffic it sends from search engines will convert. Keep doing keyword research and stay vigilant about analyzing and acting on keyword research to improve your results.

Chapter 5: Research and Brainstorm

Choose your target audience

It is difficult for a business to target each potential consumer. That is why one must select a target audience to effectively personalize online marketing and promotional messages in the correct way. Spend time to implement the following step, and it will eliminate the time and money wasted. This will then give you the time to focus on spreading your message to your customers.

Most businesses target anyone who shows interest in their service or even stay at home mum, but the following targets are general.

Targetting a specific market does not mean that you exclude the people who don't fall in that particular category. But target marketing allows one to focus on a specific market that is likely to come back and be a loyal visitor. This is something that is effective and affordable.

Check your current visitors

Determine your existing visitors and the reason why they visit your website. Look for common interests and characteristics. Find out the one with the highest sales. There is a high chance that people may benefit from a product or service.

Look out for your competition

Determine your main competitor? Don't go for the same market but you can look for a different niche market.

Analyze the features of your website

Create a list of features that set apart your website. Next to each feature, write down the benefits of each feature.

Select a specific demographic to target

This should be the moment to analyze your site analytics and define the most common demographics of people who visit your site. The demographic that you should be looking at include:

- Age
- Location
- Gender
- Income level
- Occupation
- Family status or marital status

- Ethnic background

- Education level

Consider the psychographics of your customer

Psychographics is a personal trait. This is where you determine how your site can fit into your customer lifestyle. How and when will they visit your site? What are some of the features that are highly attractive to them? Some psychographics to pay attention to include:

- Attitudes

- Behavior

- Values

- Interests

- Personality

- Lifestyles

How to find this data?

You may be wondering how you can identify this particular data from the visitors that come to your site. Well, there are different ways to do that. For example:

- Request your visitors to create a profile on your website. During that process, you can proceed to ask for questions that you want to be answered.

- Send your visitors an email with a link to a short survey.

- Provide a small pop-up window when a person leaves your site to request them to complete a short survey.

You can as well notify your site visitors that you want to improve their experience on the website. So it will be good for them to complete your survey.

What to do next

Once you have your target audience, you can decide to change your marketing strategy to help clarify your mission. You will possibly want to change your advertising efforts so that you reach out to your target market.

Find problems that you can deliver solutions

One of the most common questions that are often asked is, "What is the best way to make money as an affiliate marketer?" This question is then followed by what is the best niche to make money as an affiliate?

First, to succeed in affiliate marketing, you must identify the problems which you can deliver better solutions. This is the reason why you need to learn more and understand your target audience. If you can follow the kind of struggles which your target audience goes through, then you stand a very good chance to deliver the right solutions.

One way that you can use to help you customize your solutions to your target audience is by focusing on the best niches.

While there is no single answer on the best niche to leverage on, there are several niches which increase the possibility of you making money as an affiliate. Practically, any niche that has a lot of customers and better affiliate products to sell can be profitable in the long-run, as long as you make a smart, systematic, business-like approach to your affiliate marketing activity.

That said, categorizing different niches can be helpful in choosing your interests and strengths. After all, you must make your niche choice more profitable. The biggest mistake that most people make when selecting a profitable niche online is that they go for smaller niche markets or attempt to dive into niches that don't currently exist. These people believe that if no one is doing it can be only them who are making money on it.

The truth is that you want to dive into a big and profitable market. Competition is a healthy sign for a lot of money to be made from. So don't be scared by a niche where there are lots of people.

There are specific niches that are popular and will forever remain profitable. Let's look at those niches that you can participate as an affiliate.

1. Health

In the health market, your profitable niche can be something like treatment for wrinkle. You can even decide to narrow that down to natural wrinkle treatment and concentrate on promoting natural remedies.

Once you discover a highly specialized business area that works for you, note it down and start to concentrate on it. So let's go deep into attractive niches where you stand a great chance to earn an affiliate profit if you offer solutions.

Top 3 profitable niches

Basically, the most lucrative markets comprise of the following industries.

1. Health

2. Wealth

3. Romance

These are amazing niches.

Why?

Simply because the following industries offer what everyone is looking for.

Also, people get emotional in the following three areas.

The most profitable niches in the health industry

This is one of the most profitable niches in the world. Both the health market and the wellness market were worth $8 billion in 2018. One thing that is true is that the niches in the health never slow down people, people often look for the next best thing for health improvement, fat loss and much more.

To give you some clues of niches in the health industry that are highly profitable and popular for affiliate marketing, take time to review the list below.

1. Acid Reflux

2. Bad posture

3. Bruxism

4. Diabetic recipes

5. First Aid

6. Joint pain

7. Menopause

8. Natural Skin Care

9. Increasing the level of testosterone

10. Insomnia

11. Hair loss

12. Wrinkle treatment

13. Panic attacks

14. Nootropics

15. Vertigo

People will often be worried about different health problems. And they will never reject to test a new charm miracle pills. Additionally, the prescription fewer remedies are affordable. Anyone can buy them.

This shows the high demand for supplements and makes the market a super attractive to participate in, especially when you are an affiliate marketer and would want to gain experience and train your tactics with easy-to-sell affiliate products.

Services and products in the following niches are usually in demand because people want to look for solutions to a particular problem in their day-to-day lives. You may want to work in one or two sub-niches, to start with because it is hard to make the right offers in a sizeable broad category.

Internet marketing is a unique niche where your expertise and experience can generate money for you. If you begin a successful online business in any of the following markets, you can often build a side business that shows others how to perform it well. It can as well be a great niche where your reputation will let your niche to market high-ticket items yourself of as an affiliate.

The most profitable niches in the wealth industry

After the health and wellness industry, the next sector is the wealth market.

Wealth includes:

- Gambling

- Internet marketing

- Employment

- Business opportunities

- Stock exchange market

- And much more.

Just to show how this is a profitable niche, read the report below.

The Guardian news website reports that the online business industry is more than £100bn in the UK alone!

That is twice as big as the hotel and restaurant industry. Also, the gambling industry is vast. Based on a reliable research company, it's worth over $35.5 billion US dollars today.

So what are the best niches in the wealth industry that you can participate in?

Look at the list below:

1. App Development

2. Bitcoin

3. Affiliate marketing for busy people.

4. Coin collecting

5. ECommerce

6. Forex and trading

7. Gold Trading

8. Cryptocurrency

9. Event planning

10. Internet marketing for beginners

11. Offshore Banking

12. Online jobs

13. Penny Stocks

14. Sports Betting

15. Facebook Marketing

16. Business Startup

Next, is the Romance industry. The topmost profitable niches in the Romance and Dating Industry.

Most people won't accept it just because it is a bit intimate, but the truth is, people are of flesh and blood and are highly concerned about their family life, relationships, and intimacy.

And the real numbers can easily convince or verify the above statement. For example, the research institute StatisticsBrain reports that about 49, 250,000 people in the United States have already used online dating, and this market has proven a considerable demand.

In the romance industry, the most lucrative niches that affiliate marketing can take part:

1. Breastfeeding

2. Baby shower

3. Baby development

4. Dating to gamers

5. Dating for professionals

6. Homeschooling

7. Romance ideas

8. Senior dating

9. Wedding Planning

10. Writing poetry

11. Divorce

12. Law of attraction

13. Online dating for businesspeople over 40

14. Dating for divorced people over 40

Now you have a sense of some of the topic areas that you can decide to participate and master your affiliate marketing skills and build a consistent stream of passive income.

So far you understand that anytime you select a niche, you must ensure that it is profitable. For that reason, you must establish a routine practice and check the global worth of the market your new niche belongs to, and value rankings to monitor quality and profitability as well as verify that it deserves your effort and time.

Identify how you can deliver value

First, you must know precisely how to identify value, which you should not confuse with the price. If a consumer buys a product that means more value is placed on the products acquired than the market price. Whatever they buy is worth than their money. That makes sense, right?

So what exactly is value

Think about what it takes s to build a field of wheat, corn or whatever produce pops in mind. You need the right device and specialized machinery. The seeds have to be well watered and get rid of any pests and plagues that prevent the crops from maturing to their full potential.

In the example of cereal, once it matures, the crop requires to be harvested and then stored and refined before you can even think of distributing it to manufacturers. Next, the manufacturers have to take the grains through another set of processes, preparing the kernels to grind them afterward, then dry them and drive them through a press to mold the first flakes before you can cook.

Of course, you will get the product at a local supermarket. The whole process of growing seed and taking it from the field to storing is referred to as the Economic value chain.

Every section of the link adds value to the raw base materials.

So value is an enhancement to a product or service before it reaches the end customer.

Value added refers to instances where a company picks a product that it may consider a homogenous product with a few differences from that of a competitor, and then offer potential customers an add-on that presents a better perception of the value.

Interestingly, you can add or destroy value.

Consider the case of companies like Apple and Microsoft.

If you select an Apple product and stamp it with the Windows logo, you shall be reducing its value.

You will simply be damaging the value because Apple products are highly regarded as premium in the market. In other words, people are willing to cash in more for this particular brand than its competitors even though it might not be necessarily better.

So purpose to concentrate on the following tips to make your affiliate program successful.

1. **Develop a blueprint for communication and organization**

When you determine how an affiliate program fits into your business, it is not a one-and-done process. Building a program can be a time-intensive process, so you must plan on how you can be responsible for each development feature. Therefore, you need to come up with major metrics to focus on the progress. In case you haven't created a plan of action, it will be difficult to know when you're off track.

2. Take time to invest in the relationship with marketing advice and materials.

An affiliate program is a two-way plan. Some affiliates send prospective customers, so it is good that you take time to help them. If you can provide them with advice on how to boost traffic and optimize content would be great. Also, you should also tell them more about your products.

3. Build a brand that adds value to the consumer

When you consider the best brands in travel, insurance, property, homeware, and personal finance, know that they have a strong brand.

That is the same thing that you need to do. The value that they offer their consumers is impressive. When you have a brand that users trust, you will start to reap the benefits of affiliate marketing.

4. Build a strong ground of recurring affiliate revenue

Affiliate marketing is dynamic, that means what may work now may not work in the next month. Sometimes is because Google can update their algorithm and highly affect your affiliate programs.

There are two ways to achieve this: diversification and creation of recurring revenue.

Most affiliates focus on one-time payouts, which is good because of the inflation and the possibility to earn interest. If you earn $100 now, that is far better than $10 per month for the next ten months.

The only challenge is that a one-time payment can't guarantee you protection against major changes in your strategy. That is why it is advised to build a sizable portion of your affiliate revenue on recurring revenue.

Essentially, this method is determined by the type of niche and the products available for promotion. If the option is available, it is good to build a ground for recurring income to ensure that you have a peace of mind no matter what happens.

5. Avoid depending on a single traffic source

Back in 2011, the most successful affiliate woke up to discover that they are going to be faced out of business. This was because Google was going to release an update on their search algorithms.

The same thing happens to brands that have built up live Facebook Page audiences, and it will continue to happen every time. For that reason, it is recommended that you have a single traffic source.

Research Your Keywords and domain name

Researching something that you're passionate about is the best strategy to start, especially if you already have a community that you want to market your affiliate products.

But there are three steps to follow before settling down to a specific niche and product.

1. Be specific

Let's say you have a blog business that you are running and the most obvious niche for your affiliate efforts is SEO.

No matter how promising SEO niche may seem to be, you can't cover everything. You will simply focus on 1, 2 or even a couple of aspects of SEO, but not the entire industry. Therefore, before you can evaluate the whole potential profitability, you must split the entire topic into narrow sub-topics.

2. Evaluate your traffic potential

Now, choose between the topics you have identified, you are supposed to check whether the keyword associated with them have a significant traffic volume.

The right way to do this is to use keyword groups in the Rank Tracker.

3. Evaluate the severity of your competition

Perhaps, you don't want to compete with the brand you have no chance to outrank. So, to avoid competing with windmills, you should do your homework and verify the severity of your niche competition. Still, you can do this in the same Rank Tracker dashboard.

4. Go for a niche that is worth your effort

Next, you should not go for every low traffic niche. For some, building your content and ranking it in SERPS is easy and you should not miss that chance. On the other hand, some of the best niches may need the type of content that takes time to create, let's say they be worth it. This means you need to carefully check the pros and cons of each option, and select the ones that fit in your biz type.

Domain Name-Picking your domain name

The following steps are best if you plan to build your affiliate website from scratch. This part outlines to you a few steps that you must pay attention to:

1. A broad-industry related name vs. exact march domain for a particular keyword

This option depends highly on the long-term goals you set.

The best thing, if you plan to use the website to create your brand and build an authoritative industry resource, heading for a keyword specific domain may restrict you.

But, if you decide to pick a trend and promote a specific product, an exact match domain may be enough. Or even generate better results.

2. Product / Brand name in the domain name

Most affiliate program rules require that you use the name of the brand in your domain name. So you must be aware of buying a branded domain so that you don't get fined for infringing on a brand name.

3. The history of the domain

When asking for a domain, it is important to verify the history. This is because you don't want a domain which spammed Google with bad content. You can consider the following resources when checking out for domain.

• History of the domain in Archive.org

• The history of the domain backlinks.

Building your online presence

An online presence is vital for outbound marketing because it will boost your company and the products that you offer to the market.

It is still important inbound marketing because when you have valuable content, it will attract customers even when they aren't familiar with the brand promoted.

So what is the best thing on how you can build an online presence for affiliate marketing?

Most of the ways that you can apply to create a strong online presence have already been mentioned before. However, this section dives deep into the concept.

Create a website

The fastest and easiest way to make yourself known is through building a website. Every business deserves a website; it doesn't matter whether it is a small business or large business.

Many consumers look for products and services using the internet, and for this kind of business to remain in the industry, they must have a strong site.

Building a website is pretty simple, but you must ensure that your website has every information that your customers want.

Create an affiliate blog

Setting up a basic website is easy. Why? You can use a blogging platform like WordPress. It is a content management system that provides users with an opportunity to pay more to access a premium version.

Since WordPress can allow you to build any website, you should use it to create your affiliate blog where you can market the products and services of the partnered companies.

This will allow you to trust your target audience and build a relationship with them. Once you achieve this, you'll generate more traffic and develop an email list.

Create Informative content for your audience

For the target audience to trust and remain confident, you must deliver useful content to them.

An affiliate marketer implies that you know well the product and services that you are marketing. That is the reason why you must select your niche.

When it starts to appear like you aren't as knowledgeable as the topic you claim to be; your audience will start to lose confidence in you. You'll lose customers, and your online presence will suffer so much.

To generate quality content, you must focus on the commission you are going to create. Aim to give your audience content that is informative and one that they will benefit.

Develop a relationship and Market your products

When it is obvious that your audience trusts you, that is the time that you should start to promote your products and services. This is also the best time even to make your online presence even stronger. Below are some ways that you can market your products.

- **Review posts.** This type of posts will introduce your affiliate products to your specific audience. You can also share your insights and why they should purchase. A few points to consider include:

- Make your posts honest. Some affiliate concentrates too much on the positives of the product and prefers not to talk about the negatives. An honest review must consist of both the advantages and disadvantages. Besides, remember to use images, and other information readers can relate to.

- Your product should be something that you have tried or interested in. And make sure that your review is a deep report that will save your audience time by researching them.

- Always write your reviews in a conversational and personal tone.

- **Blog post promotion.** This is how you use your affiliate links in your own post. You must ensure that you write targeted posts when you do this.

- **Apply banners on the sidebar.** This is another great way to ensure that you receive organic and targeted traffic to your site. Putting an excellent banner is a bit difficult. So you have to make sure that your banner has all the crucial parts like a meaningful and brief message and a call to action. One of the prominent mistakes that affiliates make is placing many banners, which makes the readers confused. To prevent this, make sure that you don't have banner ads for similar services and products on your sidebar.

The function of banner ads is to suggest a particular product or service. When you place different products that serve the same purpose, your audience will have a difficult time to select which one they should get.

However, it is a smart move to incorporate banner ads for products that are relevant to a particular niche and within a specific niche. For instance, if you are writing a post on the tips for WordPress, you can attach a banner for themes, plugins, etc.

- **Social media networks**. These social platforms are also great places to market your products and services. Take, for example, Facebook; they have over a billion users. This implies that they have a large community that can generate enormous amounts of traffic that can increase sales rapidly.

If you would like to improve interactions in social media networks, make sure that you take advantage of images because people are attracted to posts that have images.

But you must be careful when selecting the images. They must be attractive and relevant to the post.

Furthermore, keep the traffic going and maintain the trust of your readers. Your social media networks should always be posted with the latest content. It must remain active and provide useful information to your readers often.

Having a strong website is the right way on how you can build an online presence for affiliate marketing. A successful affiliate marketing is one that has a strong online presence.

This will need a lot of time, hard work, patience and to continue learning, even if you have been in business for a long time.

Chapter 6: Driving High-Quality Traffic into Your Affiliate Website

Build Trust

Trust is a critical component in affiliate business. Once you have built trust with your readers or audience, then it puts your business at a better stage. If you don't know how you can create trust with your audience. Below are some tips to follow:

1. Pay attention to what your audience says

According to Edelman Trust Barometer, 62 percent of the respondents reported loving brands that listen to their questions and offers answers.

This means that if you have a blog, you should encourage them to ask questions. Then from the questions that your audience asks, respond to them. This type of personalized content goes pretty well with readers and makes them return for more. Remember that blogging is not a one-way street. You can as well create a questionnaire using Survey Monkey to receive feedback from your readers then personalize your content around the answers.

2. Offer value and purpose

You may wonder whether this is necessary. Well, if you didn't know, most successful wealthy affiliates hold this particular philosophy.

If you commit yourself to deliver a great product or service, people will want to have it no matter the price.

The same premise holds in affiliate marketing. Most affiliates fail to include value. It is not enough to post lots of content in the hope that someone is going to click one of your affiliate links. Don't sacrifice quality for quantity because both are very important. Generate content while keeping your readers in mind. This means that you recommend products which you have used. When you provide valuable content, it will help you to build your following, so make use of this as a long-term strategy.

3. Offer free products

Successful affiliate businesses offer their audience something for free. This can be an eBook or a collection of articles. By providing freebies to subscribers is a great strategy that is applied by the big names in online marketing to attract and convert readers. Grow your email list and build your community by giving.

4. Remain consistent

Affiliate marketers sometimes lose motivation to post content daily. It might not make a difference to you if you skip a post this week. But the truth is that there is a difference. It has been found that once you post between 21-54 pieces, the blog traffic will increase by up to 30%.

One great post can actually make a big difference. That means if you maintain consistency, you will gain more readers. The bottom line is it is hard to build an audience if they don't know you. The best way for you to be known is to post your content regularly.

5. Pay attention to the little details

Building trust with your audience requires that you remain careful to the little aspects of your marketing. If you are an affiliate marketer with a running blog, the little details in your site may make your readers to trust you or avoid coming to your site. Website seals are crucial factors that can determine whether you gain trust or not.

Customers don't just purchase from the business but from the people they trust. You can find success as an affiliate marketer if you find an audience and take every chance to help them.

After all, content marketing has improved ways to reach out to a broad audience that was not present in traditional marketing.

How to build an Email list for affiliate marketing?

A targeted email list is one of the oldest and effective ways of making money using affiliate marketing.

Since the email became popular, marketers have used it as a powerful tool to market their services and products. It is easy to reach out to a large audience by just sending an email.

This section will look at why an email list is the most important thing, what it can deliver to your affiliate marketing plan and how you can build one.

Affiliate marketing via email

Email is a great way that you can send information to a large number of people.

Affiliate marketing through an email is important to send out information to subscriber's email addresses. With just a piece of software, you can easily make it possible. Also, email marketing gives you the ability to send out a link so that when users click the link, they can purchase your product. Also, you will receive a commission for every affiliate program that you register. List building, which you are going to learn in this particular post, is an advanced method that you can learn and develop.

But, why is an email list important?

Let's say you have 10, 000 people who visit your niche website that promotes a specific product. That is a big number. Now, if only 100 of those people are interested in your product may be the remaining 9900 came to your site by mistake or because they clicked an ad. So out of 100 people, only a few would like to purchase your product.

You'll still be making sales but not that high.

An email list is made up of highly targeted consumers that want to read more about a product and service that you are marketing. That means if you have this person subscribed to your list, then, of course, they have some interest. If your list has 10, 000 subscribers then there is an excellent chance that a large number may buy your product or service via an affiliate link because they signed up to read your emails.

The bottom line is that email lists are a great feature of a successful affiliate marketing because they are more targeted than random visitors to your websites.

Building an email list

The next thing is how to make an email list.

Starting an email list can be as easy as having a subscribe option on your niche site where visitors can enter their email address to receive your content.

When you successfully create a list for email marketing, it means you not only develop quality content, but you need to offer something for free. You require to have an opt-in offer so that a user has to give their email address to receive the product. This can be in the form of a free eBook that is associated with affiliate marketing, a coupon code or any form of a giveaway that is related to your niche and is attractive for someone to part with their email address.

Make sure that the sign-up process is not complicated but straightforward. Don't hide it on your site but make it visible. Let it be advertised on your website that you have something that your readers would want?

Make money using an email list

Now that you are familiar with what an email list is, why is it important for you to have one? And how can you begin to build it up? How can you make money using an email list?

The answer to this is simple. Just create an impressive email content that is important to the reader. If your emails look dull, or merely contain content that is spammy, then people will quickly unsubscribe from your list.

You don't want to get into this state. You want to create an email content strategy that sells. If that is your goal, then you should avoid s sending everyday emails to your subscribers. Another thing to note is that you should not push your affiliate products and services in every email.

Just provide real, sensible and valuable content that is spaced out throughout the month. Make it a point that your email is what subscribers would want to read. And if you incorporate affiliate links to some of your emails, you'll start to see your sales increase. Why? As you send out your emails to the people who have signed up for your content, the chances are that some people are interested in buying your products.

The most important thing to remember is that you must build a relationship with your subscribers. You want them to trust you so that you don't spam them with links all the time but concentrate on giving them quality content that will make them expect your content whenever an email pops in their inbox.

Affiliate email marketing

This one of the oldest marketing strategies that people make money from, and it is still effective until today.

List building can take time and effort and is not something that you can gain overnight. A successful affiliate email marketing method is one that concerns on providing something so that the person sign up to your list. Then you can keep them subscribed by sending out regular and high-quality content. Finally, you can add in affiliate links so that they can purchase products which can change their lives.

Best Free traffic sources

To get free traffic, you must put some efforts into the work.

The best thing with free traffic sources is that once you do well in the first place, your website will gain a lot from them.

Another thing is that you don't need to spend any money on advertising. Always remember:

- You won't need to implement every single free traffic sources.

- It is important to know all the possible traffic sources.

- You must develop a habit of selecting and testing a new free traffic source.

- It is only by testing that you will find exactly the type of traffic sources that are more effective for your products.

- When you find visitors from a specific traffic source, you'll determine the details and process.

- Set up analytics tools to help you measure the traffic and performance.

Friends and connections

Look for free traffic for your website by getting in touch with your people. First, begin with your friends, clients, bloggers, people in your local community, and finally people who are in your industry.

Notify friends by sending out emails

Notify your friends by sending them an email about your new website. Their email addresses you can search from your default email. So they are your friends, people whom you know in real life, or people who you have reached out to at one point in life.

This is an effective strategy that is easy to implement. Also, it will offer your new site with an instant boost.

Notify friends with WhatsApp

Open your WhatsApp and send out to your friends a URL of your website with a message to let them know that you have released a new website. Briefly let them see what they can do on your website.

Ask friends to link from their blogs

Ask a friend with a blog to add a link under the "link exchange" or "friends" section. Since this is your friend, they won't charge you, and you may have to link back to his or her blog.

Ask friends to write a blog about your website

If you know a friend who has a blog, you can request him or her to write an article or post about your website and publish it on their blog. Again because of courtesy, you should try to link back to his or her blog.

This method can be successful for friends who have a deep relationship with you, or if your friends run a blog in the same niche as your website.

Ask your clients

If you run your own business and have clients, you can as well ask your clients to post a link on their website or mobile app to refer to their site.

Certain clients don't mind adding a link on their site to give credit to your website, especially when you have been doing a great job for them.

Ask the local bloggers

Connect with local bloggers around your city. Most bloggers who leave their contact details on their blogs. Let them be aware of your website and what you can do. Request them to let you know whether they can put a link on their blog, or write a guest post about your website.

Link up with the local community

Take time to connect with the local community. Just some examples include your local church, the brick-and-mortar store, etc. If they have a website, you can offer a service to them like:

- Provide suggestions to them about SEO

- Design a logo or some banners for them

- Advise them on how to improve SEO

In exchange, ask them to link from their sites to yours.

Make new friends from internet marketing events

Go and attend conferences or events including internet marketing. Some of these events include product events, social marketing events, and many other meetups. At these events, make it a purpose to know most of the attendees. Don't be aggressive to promote your affiliate website to them the first time you meet them, but simply exchange contact details with them, and let them know about you and your website.

Once the event is over, choose contacts who are within your niche, and ask them if they are ready to add a link on their websites. But it will take time to meet people, especially the right people and filter the best ones.

Medium

This another great resource that you can use to create a blog for free.

Best Paid Traffic sources to promote your website

Paid traffic can be the best tool for affiliate marketers. A 2017 survey by e-marketers revealed that 42 percent of small and medium businesses preferred social network ads as the best tool for marketing compared to email lists.

Below are examples of sources of paid traffic.

- Display ads.

- Social media ads.

- Paid search like Google AdWords or even Bing Ads.

- Influencer marketing.

- Sponsored content.

1. **Google AdWords**

AdWords is a traditional paid traffic source that has huge rewards, even though the cost per click is quite high. With Google AdWords, you choose keywords that you believe potential customers can search, and then you place a bid for your ad to get featured at the top of the page.

Nowadays, AdWords has evolved because of the change in online advertising. There are dynamic search ads, which personalize your ads based on the content on your website and what people are searching. AdWords also provide the ability for one to make adjustments to bids by target users or demographic group.

The more specifically you can target your AdWords, the higher the chance you will succeed. Also, Google also provides display ads on their Google Display Network.

In summary;

AdWords provide tons of ways to target and remarket, so you need to test several times until you find out the best one that works for you.

2. Outbrain amplify for advertisers

Amplify works different from AdWords or Facebook ads. First, you don't do any ads. But they provide a platform for you to post a link to your attractive content.

This is the best place to connect with your potential customers. Then you can start to provide them with valuable, funny, useful and exciting content. Just like AdWords, amplify has cost-per-click bidding system. They have a premium network of users that will make sure that your website receives traffic from a high-quality source.

3. Facebook ads

Many social media managers rank Facebook as a tool that generates the best ROI. For that reason, Facebook advertising is important for anyone who wants to pay for traffic. Facebook has many different options and keeps changing every time. They have text, images, and video slideshows. You can as well target a place, people with a specific interest or find prospects similar to a group you know already works for you. The advantage of Facebook is that it is possible to reach out precisely to who you want. You can decide to create a static or dynamic campaign.

4. LinkedIn Ads

When you deal with B2B market, LinkedIn native ads can be a good source of paid traffic. You can use it to target people who have come to your website. Target them by contact, by Title, geography, and industry. They offer options such as display ad, sponsored feeds and InMail ads.

5. Twitter Ads

Twitter is another great place to use to market your affiliate business and drive paid traffic. Experts in Twitter can drive a massive organic traffic. Twitter supports promotion of a single tweet, a trend, and pay per click.

Actionable tips to succeed in affiliate marketing

Affiliate marketing is a great source for one to make income. The secret to succeeding as an affiliate is to provide an additional value to your readers.

Traditional ads used to pay for impressions or clicks. If a user signed up for a newsletter using a given link, then affiliates could earn a profit. No matter what, you can't be paid until when you have made your readers to take a specific action.

That said, these are the best tips that affiliate marketers should use to increase the chances of success.

1. Know your target audience

The best methods for one to use affiliate networks is to market products, services, and offers that rhyme with the needs and wants of the audience. Ask yourself why they are coming to your site, signing up for your email marketing list, or even following you on social media.

In case you write description of tech products, don't attach ads for soccer balls. But you can customize the ads on your audience. The more relevant the ads appear, the more likely they will click them. An exciting way to take a look at affiliate marketing is to teach your audience about the services and products they are interested in.

Not only does learning about your audience gives you a better chance to sell your products, but it can as well help you know the best places to advertise, market and promote your website to drive more traffic.

The more information you have about your audience, the better you can use demographics, and other information to target your audience when advertising on social platforms.

The bottom line is to make sure that you market products that are directly relevant to your audience. The more relevant your ads, the more sales you'll make.

2. Establish trust

A lot has been said about this. Just to emphasize, readers are known to be savvy. They can identify an affiliate link once they see one. So if you mess around and destroy the trust by sending them many ads or marketing a product that you don't have much trust in, they will leave and never come back.

Don't forget that repeat visitors are the ones that will drive traffic for you. These are responsible for link back and recommendations. That is why you need to build that trust and maintain it all through.

If your visitors believe that you are not honest or they start to think that you are only recommending products and services because you have the motive to make money, they will not read anything that you post for them.

If you market products of low quality, they will lose trust in your recommendations and stop to act on them, and your sales will go down.

With this in mind, you want to ensure that you remain the priority in their minds. So make sure that you only share products that are relevant to them.

Additionally, it is good to disclose any affiliate relationship that you have with your vendors. Most people are fine with this, and the increased level of transparency can help you expand your business.

3. Be helpful

Look at affiliate ads as an extra tool that adds value to your content. Add value to your content by ensuring that it is informative, useful and educative.

Avoid creating a list of best books and hope that people will be interested to click the affiliate link to buy the books. But take time and write a comprehensive review, then you can use the affiliate ads to point in the right direction if they decide to work on the information.

In case you have a personal testimony or case study, you can share it out with them. Write a comprehensive post about it and share with them.

Remember the main idea is to deliver useful content that adds value to the life of the visitors.

4. Be transparent about your affiliate relationships

Your readers love when you become transparent. Being honesty will lead to an increase in your earnings. When readers start to sense that you are telling the truth about your connections, they are smart enough to bypass all your links and move to the next vendor.

So honesty and transparency are important if you want to have a loyal reader base. They are aware that they provide you with the support by clicking on the referral links. Therefore, you must make them happy to do so.

In some cases, you can decide to offer a bonus or some type of incentive if they take action and use your website.

When we have a lot of affiliates promoting the same vendor, a bonus is the best way to make them want to buy directly from you.

5. Choose your affiliate products carefully

Before you select your affiliate products, find time to research all the different products and services affiliate networks offer. Figure out the types of products your readers may want. You can also change the ads and test different types, and only apply different graphics and text to define the most effective ones.

It can take time before you figure out the correct formula, and you may discover that you require to rotate ads to impress more visitors.

In most cases, the people who created the product will offer you some ads to use on your site, social media platform, and email. Try out different ad creative to find out the ones that work for you best.

You may as well want to set up your own ads to find out how it stands out from the rest.

One thing that you should not forget to do is to market digital information products. These type of products are attractive for two reasons. First, they feature a better conversion rate because the customers receive immediate access and instant satisfaction when they buy. Secondly, they have a better rate of commission than physical products; this means more profit for you.

Besides this, make a purpose of promoting high priced products and products that renew monthly to receive a higher commission and monthly commissions. Receiving a monthly recurring affiliate sale is a better way to make income in your affiliate business more stable and predictable.

6. Create timeless content

Content that was written a long time ago can as well be useful although it doesn't appear on your page. Utilize the long-term profits by delivering timeless content.

When visitors find your old content and discover that is was written a long time ago, it may turn them away. To solve this, you can add links to your updated posts on your old content.

Regularly updating your older posts is the best way to maintain and improve your SEO ranking. Many platforms nowadays give you the opportunity to highlight "most recent" or "related articles" on each page. And don't forget that your old content can still generate earnings for you.

While writing new and latest information can be useful, another method is to concentrate on writing "evergreen" content.

This will provide you with an added advantage and drive traffic for years to come, and you have the chance to change up the products you are marketing associated with the content.

The main thing here is to have content that is relevant, useful and up-to-date. You may have to go with both strategies in your content. Lastly, you can pull out the dates from your blog posts. This means that although the content could have been written a long time ago, the information is still relevant. Many people tend to ignore relevant but old content. So deleting the dates makes the content relevant to these particular group of people.

7. Remain patient

Revenue from affiliate marketing grows and increases with time. There are special programs that have a lifetime payout. If you direct a visitor to sign up for a given program, you can continue to receive money from that visitor even if he or she doesn't come to your site.

If you concentrate on marketing recurring billing products, there is a possibility to continue to earn commissions each month on the same products which can increase with time.

Affiliate programs aren't a means to become rich quickly, but it offers the right chance to make passive income from your site. While you continue to add more content to your website, market more services, and products, increase traffic to your website, and build your email marketing list, you'll continue to expand the affiliate marketing side of your business and make more money.

8. Stay relevant

You need to stay updated with the latest offers of your affiliate networks. New tools, ads and always improved to increase usability and appeal to customers. Little changes tend to motivate readers. So make sure you embrace the changes that happen every day. Don't be left out in the dust.

Don't be lazy to the point where you don't follow trends and explore new opportunities. For example, if a given diet or clothing is not popular, you may decide to remove that content and recommendation from your site, or even update your post to reflect that.

Make sure that you are on the lookout for new products, especially the ones that relevant to your niche. The more products you market, the more money you can make.

9. Try different programs

When you find out that a given program is not working, then you should try another one. Affiliate programs are different. They have different services, products, and payment systems.

Some programs offer a lifetime payout on sales while others have limit of between 3-90 days. Search for your favorite vendors and find out about their affiliate program. Try and incorporate systematic ad testing into your strategy to utilize any benefits.

When you continually test different programs, you will start to see the ones that have the best conversion rates and the ones that users respond to most.

Another strategy that you can apply is to negotiate high payouts with affiliate programs where you have a good track record. Many vendors are happy to reward affiliates who have a high commission.

10. Content should be first

Make sure that your content marketing strategy is your priority.

Your content should be your solid rock, the foundation on which your site runs. Without useful and relevant content, readers won't visit your website. So you must focus on creating high-quality content for your readers and monetizing your strategies.

Remember that when you compromise your content, then that would be the start of you losing readers. Once it happens, you won't get the chance to earn from your ads.

We can't stress more than that, the quality of your content will be the single most factor in boosting the credibility of your affiliate site.

Conclusion

Affiliate marketing is an industry that keeps changing, and for that reason, you must always be ready to explore new possibilities. It is important to discover new opportunities for you to increase your income.

For individuals who are thinking of setting up an affiliate marketing, think no more. The internet is a great platform where you can make your business succeed as well as compete with the rest. You only need to have a great website and convert it into a profitable one.

Before you move on to sign up for an affiliate network, it is better if you already have an existing website that generates a steady flow of web traffic. This will give you an upper hand because you already have an audience on the internet.

To boost your position as a prospective partner, make sure you include effective marketing techniques such as brand marketing, search engine optimization, social media marketing, and influencer marketing.

Above all, make sure that you create relevant and quality content. Also, your content should address the needs of your audience. You can make a huge profit from affiliate marketing but only when you are patient and committed to following the right path. Remember. Many people have joined affiliate marketing, but only a few are enjoying the profits that come with affiliate marketing. So be smart and focus on giving your audience value. Over time, you will start to reap the many benefits that come with affiliate marketing.

Finally, if you found this book useful in any way, a review on Amazon is always appreciated!

SEO Mastery

Learn Advanced Search Engine Optimization Marketing Secrets, For Optimal Growth! Best Beginners Guide About SEO For Keeping your Business Ahead in The Modern Age!

Graham Fisher

Table of Contents

Introduction

Times are changing and the internet is becoming the main way to add success to your business. Whether you write a blog or own a restaurant, you need your online profile to represent the greatness of your brand. You also need people to find your information from online searches. If you own a children's toy store, you want your results to come up not only when people search "the best toy store" but also when they search the best places to shop in your specific city. You especially want to make sure that your business shows up in the search results when people are searching specifically for you.

So, how can you make sure these things are happening? You need to learn all about SEO, or Search Engine Optimization. Search engine optimization makes sure that when people are searching online, they find your business right where you want them to. It ensures the searches that display the best sides of your company allow you to show up in the results. It can also ensure that you get to be at the very top of the page.

In this book, we are going to take you from not knowing much about search engine optimization to being a complete SEO expert. We are going to share what SEO is, how you can do it, and what results come from what actions. We will answer all of your big questions and we will explain things that you may not even yet know exist. We will give you the tips and the tricks you need to optimize your business's SEO to your very best ability.

If you are ready to become an SEO expert, you have come to the right place. We are excited to help you learn and we know that our book is the very best resource to learn all about search engine optimization.

Chapter One: What is Search Engine Optimization?

The first thing we need to learn while we are looking into how to best represent your business in search results is what exactly search engine optimization is. To start with this topic, let's look into how Google works.

So to start, we all know that Google started its days as simply a search engine. This is the part of the Google company that we need to learn about, so as we refer to Google, we will be referring to its search engine capabilities.

Google works by using algorithms based on what you type into its search bar. It also uses things called spiders, or crawlers, to search for information all over the internet. The main thing that Google runs on, however, is something called Keywords. Keywords are the main base of search engine optimization and they are something that you will completely master creating by the end of this book. We will look into keywords in great detail in the next chapter, learning what they are, why they are important, and exactly how to use them to benefit you and your business as much as possible. For now, just remember that they are extremely important in the way that Google works.

Another thing that is important in how Google works is that it looks into how long websites have existed. If your website has been around for years, it has a much better probability of showing up in a Google search than a website that was just created yesterday. Google does this because websites are easy to create and surprisingly, new websites are actually created every single day from all around the world. Some of these websites become a big deal. Think of Facebook, for example. One day it was just a brand new website. A few years later, it was something that everyone in the world knew about and something that most people in more privileged countries use on a daily basis. Other websites, however, maybe like the nutrition blog your old high school classmate started on a whim, will be posted to three or four times and then forgotten about and/or given up on. Google needs to tell the difference between these two types of sites, which shows why it matters not only how good your site is, but also how long it has been around online.

Google also looks into how much traffic, or how many people are clicking on and visiting your online site, your webpage is getting. A website that has only been clicked on three hundred times is much less relevant to what a person is searching for than a website that has been vied many millions of times. When people search on Google, they are usually looking for accurate results and usable information. If a site has been clicked on many times, Google knows that the information it has is useful and relevant.

Lastly, Google also looks at how many other sites online have clickable links that direct viewers to the website. If your site is referred to by many other websites and there are many links out there that direct right to your site, Google knows that people online like your information. They know that people refer you as a great source, which allows them to believe that you are a great source as well. This is actually the best way to get your site to show up in Google searches because they put so much trust in your website when other real people continue to refer it and advertise it.

So far we know that Google works through keywords, the age of websites, how much traffic a website gets, and how many links direct to a website. These things all make sites show up higher in search results and without these things, results are obviously much lower. It is also important to note, however that Google keeps some secrets as to how it works as well. It is definitely the best search engine available and everyone who uses the internet knows this. If Google gave away all of their secrets and every piece of how their search engine worked, other search engine sites would be able to copy them. They would then no longer stand out as the top search engine, so of course they cannot share all of their information with us.

These are the most commonly used ways in which Google ranks websites for their search results, but let's look into the entire top ten ranking factors that they use as well. We can never have too much information on how Google works, because we want our website to fit exactly what they are looking for in order for it to show up as a top result.

1. The first ranking factor for Google is making sure that your website is safe and secure. It cannot have links to viruses or other malicious sites or software, because people trust google to only bring them to safe sites. Google needs to keep up this reputation by not listing sites that are not safe and secure. In this same category, your site also needs to be easy to access. If it is a website that people cannot see or people have a hard time seeing, this hurts Google's reputation as well. People want results that will help them, not things that they cannot see. Because of this, Google

will not rank your site high if it is not easily accessible.

2. The second thing that Google looks into is the speed of your website. People do not like to wait a long time for things to load. Because of this, your website needs to be quick in order to show up well in Google search results.

3. The third thing Google looks into is that your site is able to be viewed well on mobile devices. This is because almost all of the web surfing that happens today is happening on smartphones. People still use computers often, but the typical simple Google search is done on phones more often than not. If your website only loads well on a computer screen and is difficult to use from a smartphone, it will not rank high in Google search results.

4. The fourth thing that Google looks into is how long your website has been around on the internet, which we looked into previously.

5. The fifth thing that Google looks into on your site is how relevant and useful your information is. If your information does not match the searches, it obviously will not show up in the results. For example, if you have a pizza parlor your website will not show up

when someone searches for "dog groomer near me".

6. Google of course also looks into technical SEO. We will discuss this in great detail later, but it involves keywords, web analytics, and other technical features of the search engine results.

7. The experiences that users of Google have on your site is important as well. Google uses a site called RankBrain to see what people around the world think of different websites. The ones that are well-enjoyed will show up in the top search results while the ones with bad reviews or no reviews will not show up well.

8. As well mentioned earlier, links that lead to your website are extremely important as well. This detail has a heavy weight in Google's decision on where to rank your site.

9. Social signals are important to Google. This includes the amount of traffic, or visitors, that view your site as well mentioned earlier as well as how your site does on social media, which we will look into in great detail later in the book.

10. The last thing that Google looks into while they are ranking your site is that you have information about a real business. If your site

leads to a real place, it will show up much higher in search results. This tool is especially important to pay attention to when you are creating a site that you want people to find who are local and close to you, which we will also look into in great detail in another chapter of this book.

The reason why we need to know how Google works is because it helps us to ensure that our results rate well in every category that they look into. Now, let's look into some things that used to help in search engine optimization but are no longer useful at all.

The first thing that people used to do but should no longer do, is to add many links to your web content just to look better to Google. Google has changed to look at the quality of your links and not the quantity of them. If your site links to ten small sites that have little to no traffic, it will not show up in search results as well as a site that has two great, highly visited sites linked into their content.

This also means that if your twenty mom-blog friends link to your website, it may not help you very much in terms of your SEO. However, if you get a link to your site from a well-known company, this will help your SEO greatly.

The next thing that people used to focus on but should not anymore is making sure they always have the number one spot on Google. Google today is filled with ads, so even if you are the number one result, you may not show up at the top of the page. This also means that people are more likely to scroll down and pick the result they find the most helpful or interesting. Because of this, you are just as well off if you appear in the top five results rather than going out of your way and wasting time, energy, and resources to be the number one.

It is also important to remember that your main goal is to make a website that people like and that they can benefit from. It needs to represent your business well. If your site does not do this, it does not matter where you show up in search results. You may have high traffic, but people will leave your site quickly if it is not helpful or enjoyable.

Because of this, do not focus too much on SEO. If SEO is the only thing you focus on, you may forget the purpose of your website. If you forget your purpose, you will have a great SEO result and a website that no one likes.

People also used to make sure that their websites were huge with many pages and a large amount of information. If you do this, you may forget to make posts that are again useful and that people enjoy. This is an area where quality is much more important than quantity. A few useful posts and pages are much better and more appreciated that one hundred sites that do not have the information that people are looking for.

Also, you need to be careful with your keywords. Logically, more keyword usage will make your results show up higher in Google. However, if you use your keyword too often, it will be difficult for readers to understand your content. If you use your keyword incorrectly, it will definitely turn people away.

Overall, when you are building a website today you need to pay more attention to the people who will be visiting it than the SEO. Of course you still need to use SEO tools to help people find your site easily and quickly, but use them tastefully. This is a switch in mindset from how SEO used to be used. It is, however, a very important thing to understand.

Another thing to pay attention to when working on your SEO are the three pillars of SEO success. These include Authority, Trust, and Relevance. These three pillars mean exactly what you probably think they mean. Authority means that you need to ensure that your audience (and Google) believe that you are a person that they should listen to about the topic you are writing about. Do you own the business that the page is for? Do you have a doctorate degree in the subject being discussed? Do you have many years of experience in the business or topic being discussed?

If so, you have the authority to speak on that topic or business. For trust, you simply need to make sure that what you are writing can be trusted. Is your information from personal experience? Do you cite sources or include links to where you found the information? Is your writing honest and are your reviews truthful? If so, your readers (and Google) can trust you. Lastly, relevance makes sure that the topics you write about on your site go along with the information people are searching for. For example, if you have a food blog and people come to you for recipes, post about food and not articles about horses or something else completely unrelated. Following these three pillars of success will help you SEO and will keep readers happy with your website.

It is also extremely important to note when speaking of Google, that their algorithms change and their website updates. It is very important to stay ahead of these updates. If a big update takes place and things change drastically, your SEO could suffer. To avoid this, pay attention to the news on this topic. Follow along with reported upcoming updates and research them to see if they are real. If they are, be ready to change things up to optimize SEO in the latest way possible.

Chapter Two: Keyword Research– The Most Important Step of SEO

As we mentioned at the very beginning of our book, keywords are the most important thing to know about and to use correctly when looking into your search engine optimization (SEO). In this chapter, we will look into keywords in detail. We will discuss what keywords are, why keyword research is so important, how to find keywords, how to use keywords, and more.

First, let's figure out what a keyword actually is. A keyword is a word that explains your article. It is a word that when someone types it into the Google search bar, you would like your article to be in one of the top spots in the result list. It is a word that when searched, your webpage would be an accurate result that would give searchers the exact information that they were looking to find.

Next, let's look into why keywords are important. Keywords are the sole way that Google decides what searches will lead to your page. The other factors that Google uses determines your ranking within the results, but your keywords are the reason why you are found in that specific list at all. Without keywords, you would not turn up in the right search results. You would not be found where you want your readers to find you. Google would not know if your content was relevant to your main subjects.

Overall, keywords are your way to have control over where you show up in search engine results. They allow you to appear in certain searches and not in others, and they put the control of this in your own hands. If you do not take action over this control, your SEO will suffer greatly.

So, let's look into how you can use this tool to your fullest ability. First of all, you need to do research on your keywords. Researching your keywords allows you to see what other results come up with the keywords that you are thinking of using. You can do this type of keyword research by simply typing in your word or phrase into the Google search bar and looking at the list of results.

You can do another type of keyword research as well. You can use certain websites and type in your keyword, and they will help you to know which keyword will generate the most traffic to your site. One site like this is moz.com.

Another way to tell if a keyword is good or not is to buy a sample campaign from a site like Google AdWords. This would basically be buying an advertisement that would show up based on the keyword that you chose. You could make the traffic that came from clicking the ad redirect to your website. By doing this, you would be able to tell how much traffic was generated by the keyword and if it was useful or not.

Next, let's look into how you can find and choose keywords. First, a good way to find keywords is to use an online tool that will help you to generate a massive list of them. One of these tools is again within GoogleAdWords. In this program, there is a keyword tool. This tool will make a huge list of keywords for you. It will also tell you how much traffic is typically generated from each keyword. Keywordtool.io is another option for keyword research. This site is nice because when you type in your keyword, it allows you to click on different sites like YouTube and Amazon to see how well your keyword would work. This makes the tool usable not only for Google results but videos and selling products as well.

These tools can not only be used to find keywords that will work for you, but also to ensure that the keywords you choose will make traffic come to your site. As we mentioned earlier, they can tell you which keywords bring traffic to your site and approximately how much traffic they can bring as well.

We mentioned earlier in the book that Google ranks your content based on how relevant it is to its searches, but how does it do this? How does Google know what you website is even about? Let's look into these questions and figure out how we can optimize our SEO in this way.

The way that Google knows what your web page is about is through On Page SEO. On Page SEO is search engine optimization techniques that show on your website, not external links. External links help to your Google result rankings, but On Page SEO tells Google what you are talking about.

Let's now look into the different types of On Page SEO. The first and most important component in On Page SEO is the content of your site. It's what the person searching is actually looking for, so it is what Google puts the biggest emphasis on.

Next, On Page SEO needs a title tag. A title tag is something that shows up in the web address and it is also what will show up on Google as the title of the website. You need a good title tag so that Google can rank you higher and so that people can see an interesting title to click on when they see your search engine result.

The next thing that a good On Page SEO needs is an acceptable URL. The URL should tell the reader what the website is going to talk about. If it simply has a chain of random letters and numbers, it will not rank as high on Google and will not be as well understood by your site visitors.

Now that we have looked at On Page SEO, let's look into how you can structure your web page for easy and automatic SEO. We all know that running a business or a webpage can be hard work. If anything can be done automatically for you or at least easily by you, it can be a big help.

Before we look into how to structure your site, though, let's look into why this is so important. The first reason why the structure of your site is important is because it makes a good experience for the people who visit your site. This is important because the more people that are happy with your site, the more people will visit it and possibly even help you out by linking to your pages.

Also, if your structure is set up right, your Google search result will have site links listed. This is when your main page is listed as a Google result, but in smaller form underneath this result are links to your other pages. This not only makes your Google result look more professional, but helps visitors to get to the place they want or need easily as well, which in turn optimizes user experience again.

Remember how we talked a little bit about how Google uses spiders, or crawlers, in the beginning of our book? Well, if your site has a good structure, these spiders of crawlers are able to navigate your web page better and find more information, which allows you to rank higher in Google results without much effort on your part.

Now that we know why site structure is so important, let's learn what you really want to know. How can you structure your site for optimal SEO? First, you will want to make a type of hierarchy with your site information. This means that you will start with your main page, and that main page will have a few segments to other pages of your site. These other pages with have links to a few of your other pages which will have links to a few other pages and so on. It is almost like building a pyramid. You start with the broadest and most important information and let things trickle down the line. The most important thing to remember when you are building your pyramid is to make sure that your order makes sense. Then, make sure that your number of pages or articles is not overwhelming. Consider keeping more than two but less than seven links to main categories from your home page. Lastly. Make sure that the number of subcategories that each category has is an equal or somewhat equal number. For example, do not have one category have two subcategories and the other category have ten subcategories.

Another thing to pay attention to when building the structure of your website is the structure of your URL. Just as it is important that your URL is readable and makes sense, it is also important that your URL follows the structure that your web page follows. This will help Google to understand the structure of your site and it will make for a better user experience at the same time.

Something called a shallow depth structure in regards to navigation is important as well. This means that to access the information on your site, visitors should need to click only one, two, or three times. If they have to click more times than this, it may be difficult to find information or it may even feel confusing. This also makes those Google crawlers or spiders be able to find your information much easier, which helps it to show up higher in search results.

It is also important to have a header that includes clickable links to your main categories on your site. This header should stay the same no matter what page of the site you are viewing. These headers are the types of menus that optimize SEO. Other menus like side menus or drop down menus do not help SEO at all, even if they may look nice on your site.

You can also use internal links on your web page. When you use internal links, it will help to make more traffic visit multiple pages on your site instead of just the one they initially set out to view. It will also show Google that your pages are being linked to, which is again the most important factor in how Google ranks you in their search engine results. Yes, it even counts when you link to your own information!

These ways of structuring your site are important to think about whether you are just now building your page or if you are rearranging your site in order to have better SEO. If you follow these structure tips, your search engine rankings are sure to be higher than they would be otherwise.

Next let's look into how to make Google notice your keywords. You use many words in your article, so how does Google know which ones to pick up as keywords for your SEO? Well, you will need to know about keyword placement in order to help yourself in this area. It is helpful if you put a keyword in your first paragraph and in your last paragraph in order for Google to notice them. You can also pay attention to your keyword density. This is the percentage of keywords you use in comparison to the rest of the words you use in your article. The best keyword density is typically between one and three percent. This allows Google to notice your keywords, but keeps your writing readable for your site visitors at the same time.

Now that we have covered how you can get your website to show up well in Google rankings, let's figure out how you can get people to actually click on the link to your site. We have already mentioned some things that can help in this area. First, make sure that you have a strong, intriguing title tag. This is what people pay the most attention to, so if it is a good title, more people are likely to click on your site in their Google search.

Next, you will need to make sure that your URL is set up nicely. You want your URL to be both readable and in a logical order. This is something that may look at in their google result as well, so it is important for it to be something that looks relevant and of high quality.

Site Speed is important for your Google ranking as well. Of course, site speed is important to your viewers. This allows viewers to enjoy your site and to possibly, and hopefully, even link to it. Why is it important to Google, though? Well, this again goes back to those crawlers or spiders. The faster your site is, the faster the crawlers or spiders can look through the information. The more information they find, the higher you will show up in the Google rankings, which in turn optimizes your SEO.

Next we will look into duplicate content versus original content. Original content helps your SEO and duplicate content hurts your SEO. This is because if you have the same information as another site or extremely similar information to another site, Google does not really know which one to rank above or below the other one. If you have completely original content, Google does not have a problem separating you from other results. This will avoid you having to have potentially lower SEO results for a great page just because someone else has a page with similar information.

Usability is an important thing to keep in mind when trying to optimize your SEO as well. It's kind of difficult to see why SEO and usability are related, since usability is something that is experienced by visitors after they have already found and gotten to your web page. However, it truly is important. It's important because good usability keeps people coming back to your site and even may make people refer you or link to your content. These things will not happen if your site is difficult to use. Because of this, if your site is easier to use, it will positively affect your SEO.

As we mentioned earlier in the article, mobile support is very important to SEO as well. This is because most people today browse the internet on their smartphones. This makes your web page useless if they are not able to view it from their mobile devices. Google knows this as well and they take this into account when ranking you in the search engine results.

Google not only rates your site with online algorithms and spiders and crawlers, but with human raters as well. These raters look at your web pages and judge them based on Google's search quality guidelines. These guidelines do update, so it is important to stay on top of what they are so that you can optimize your SEO with these human raters as well as the online ones. There are over 10,000 of these people who rate search engine results around the world. Google contracts with them to have their help in their ranking system. These raters are given words or phrases to search, and then they rate and rank the results that show up. This allows Google to ensure that real people are happy with the results that their computers are creating, and allows them to change the results if the real people are not happy with them.

One important thing to think about when looking into Google's search quality guidelines and human ranking team is that they look not only into your website and the information you have on it, but also into you as the author or creator of the site. This makes it more important than ever for you to have an "about me" section on your website. If you do not have this section about yourself or if it does not make you seem both credible and interesting, your SEO results may fall because of it.

This helps Google to make sure that authors and creators of sites are credible. This helps them with the amount of fake news that has been spreading online lately. Google wants to spread true information, and this is part of their way to do so.

Another thing that these human raters check for is that sites actually have interesting and useful information that relates to the word or phrase being searched for. Many sites today just write with many keywords to make their page show up in Google without making their information beneficial at all. Google discovered this and is fixing that problem with their search quality guidelines and human raters.

These are just a couple of the Google search quality guidelines. Make sure to stay up to date on these guidelines to ensure that your web page has optimal SEO, because the guidelines do seem to change frequently.

Next, let's look into readability. This is one of those topics that is again difficult to see affecting SEO because it is something that users experience after they actually get to your site, not when they are choosing it from search engine results. However, just like the usability, readability keeps visitors coming back to your site. It may make them refer others to your site or may make them even link to your site in their own pages.

SEO also works very well with content marketing. Content marketing is making sure you have the right content on your site for the type of users you want to attract. It is made up of a target audience, valuable content, and promotion through things like ads. All of these tactics bring traffic to your site, which in turn betters your SEO. They also make your site more useful and usable, which again helps your SEO.

Google also uses something featured snippets. These are the results that they choose to feature in small amounts at the top of the search result page. If you get featured in these snippets, it can help your SEO and cause you to have significantly more traffic. Let's look into how you can get your page featured in these snippets.

First, you need to figure out which searches make Google snippets show up, as not all searches do this. Sometimes, they show up when the user enters a question into the search bar. Making sure your page comes up from searching a question that your site answers may be able to get you into the snippets section. To decide what questions to ask, think about your audience. What types of questions do you think they have?

We could easily say "Wow" about how much of a difference keywords make and how many different things go into your Google search result rankings. Let's make a checklist of things you should do or add in order to see your site show up toward the top of the page in search engine results.

- Use well-researched and effective keywords
- Pay attention to keyword placement and density
- Use title tags
- Have a clear, structures URL
- Put your site menu in your header
- Give your site a logical structure
- Pay attention to your site load speed
- Make sure you are not displaying duplicate content- from your site or another site
- Make sure your site is usable and readable
- Pay attention to mobile friendliness
- Stay up to date on Google's search quality guidelines
- Write strong content, not just keywords
- Consider using content marketing
- Try to get featured in Google snippets by using question keywords

If you do these things, your SEO should be better than ever. These tips will help you to get to the top few spots in Google search results. They will increase the traffic to your site therefore boosting your business or web page. Make sure you know the information in this chapter well and refer back to it as you are creating or restructuring your site. These tips and tricks and things that are easy to do, but come with a big reward.

Chapter Three: Link Building– How to Rank Extremely High on Google

So far in this book, we have mentioned many ways in which you can optimize your SEO and make your web page show up higher in the Google search results. Do you remember, though, what the very best way to raise your search engine result ranking was? That's right, the best way to raise your rank in the search results is through links. Both having links to strong content and being linked to from other websites helps your SEO greatly. In this chapter, we are going to look into something called link building. We will talk about what link building is exactly, a dirty little secret that no one tells you about link building, how to use link building and how not to use it, and more.

First, let's look into what link building really is. Link building is the process that you use to get other websites and their authors to link to your page. Remember, this is the factor that Google gives the most power to when ranking you in their search engine results, so it really is very important if you want your SEO to be successful. Building links both brings new visitors to your site and therefore adds to your traffic, and also adds to your level of authority when Google looks into your page. It shows that other people on the internet like your information and that they trust you. It shows that your content is beneficial, useful, and readable. It proves to Google that you probably have many of the important SEO factors, because people would not link to you if you did not have these.

It is important to know that there are two ways to get people to link to your site and that they are definitely not equal in their benefits. The first way that you can get linked to is to purchase backlinks. You can go online and pay a person or company to link to your site. This process is not ideal and should be avoided if possible. This can make you have links to your site that are from low quality places. It can even get your site blocked or banned for using this method of backlinking. This is because Google wants their results to actually be useful and have real authority, not authority that you can purchase on the internet.

The way that you should get people to link to your site is called the natural way. This process is difficult and it takes time and maybe even a little bit of luck, but it helps your SEO greatly so it is very worth it.

It is also important to note that even though you are getting links naturally, not all links are as helpful as others. Links give you better credibility when they are put in a larger website that has great SEO. If you get linked to in a site like National Geographic, for example, this would be huge. Not only does National Geographic have a huge following and list of readers that would possibly click on your link and be turned into your traffic, but they are also a big, trustable source in the eyes of Google. When Google sees you linked to popular or well-visited websites, they give you a higher ranking in their search results that if you were linked to in a smaller, less visited page.

Think about if instead of being linked to in National Geographic, you were linked to in your cousin's parenting blog that has about twelve trusted followers. This would cause much less traffic to visit your site through clicking the link, if any at all. Your cousin's blog also isn't a source that Google knows as credible, so it would not heighten your SEO results even close to as much.

It is important to remember, however, that any natural link is better than nothing. These links are still factored into your Google rankings. Even if it just a link from a small business in your area, it is much better than having no links at all in terms of your SEO.

So, link building is very important as you can see. It is important because it brings new visitors to your site. It is also important because it improves your credibility in the eyes of Google, which in turn allows you and your site to rank higher within their billions of results.

Next, let's look into a dirty little secret that typically no one would tell you about link building. We are telling you this because we want you to succeed, so we are giving you every piece of information that we have and every piece of knowledge that you will need in order to be extremely successful with your SEO. The big secret in link building is that Google is watching what you are trying to do. They are watching you and they are trying to stop you. Google knows that people have come up with strategies to be linked to in another peoples' content. This is not something they want. They want their results to be completely natural and they do not want you to have control over their systems. Because of this, pay attention to the tools and tricks that Google knows about and avoid them. For example, buying links actually used to work until Google found out and made it a process that you want to avoid at all costs. Pay attention to Google and what they are doing at the time. This changes all the time, so you will need to search often to stay updated.

Next, let's look into a linking tool called anchor text. When you put a link in your web page, you can decide if you want that link to simply show the URL of the source or if you want it to appear as something else that can be clicked on. You can make any words a clickable link with this tool. Anchor text allows you to put links in your content without losing its readability. It also is an easy way to tell people what they link is about, as well as an easy way to give them the site you are referring to just as they are reading about it and actually need it. Anchor text also looks much more professional that a clickable link that displays an entire URL in the middle of your web page content.

Anchor text also helps your SEO. The words that you choose to use for your clickable link tell Google what the content of the link is about. They use the words that you use for the link in order to decide what the content of the link actually is without ever needing to go to the linked site.

Anchor text also has the ability to show up at the end of a link's URL. When the text shows up here, it allows the URL to show what the content of the link is. Google can use this information to tell what the linked site is about as well.

There are six different types of anchor text that you can use or that you want others to use when linking to your site. Let's look into these six types of anchor text now.

- Exact–Match: This type of anchor text displays the exact same keyword that is used for the page that is being linked to. This ensures that it tells the reader what the link will be about.
- Partial–Match: This includes words that are similar to the keyword on the page being linked to, but not the exact same word or phrase. It still shows what the site will be about, however, just not in such an exact and precise way.
- Branded: This type of anchor text shows the name of the site or brand that is being linked to.
- Naked Link: This is simply using the URL and not choosing a specific word or phrase.
- Generic: This type of anchor text would say something along the lines of "click here".
- Images: The source for images that are sites are typically put in anchor text fashion, allowing readers to click on the links to see where the photo came from and allowing for the writers to give credit to the photographers.

When you are using anchor text, there are some important things to remember, This does not necessarily benefit your SEO, but it benefits the link that you are using and that person's SEO. If you benefit another person's SEO, they may want to help you as well. Because of this and just because it is the kind thing to do, you should make sure that your anchor text is made in the best way possible to allow it to get as many clicks as possible.

To make the best anchor text, make sure that it is a word or short phrase. If the phrase you use for the anchor text is too long, it may not look professional, may decrease readability, or may make less people actually go through and click on the link. You also need to make sure that the content you are linking to is relevant and useful. Random anchor text links to unrelated or unhelpful sites will only decrease the user approval rate of your own site, which in turn would hurt your SEO.

It can also be a good idea to consider not using a person's keyword when linking to their article. If people continually link to your web page with the same exact keyword, Google may notice this and they may think that you bought the links. Of course, this would not be natural link building so it would hurt your SEO greatly.

Now that we have learned all about links, what they are, what they do, and why they are important, let's look into how you can start link building and getting other people on the internet to link to your site. We will start by looking into some beginner strategies in the link building field.

One of the easiest link building strategies is to simply ask people you know if they could link to your site on their web page. You can ask family members or friends who have a blog or you could even ask local businesses that are in a related field to your content. You need to be a little bit careful with this strategy, because you only want related and relevant sites to link to your content. If your website is for selling crocheted items, you probably don't want links from a dentist office in an article that talks about taking care of your teeth, for example.

If your website is for a business, another thing that you can do to get a link is to list yourself on the Better Business Bureau. When you do this, the website will show a link to your site. This is an expensive way to get just one link, but it's a strategy to start with and a Better Business Bureau listing may even help your business anyway.

Also consider following along with other blogs that are similar to your website or your content. If you comment on their blogs often, they may start to notice you. They may then check out your page and they may like it and someday even decide to link to it. This is not a way that has guaranteed results, but it is a beginner strategy that is definitely at least worth a try.

If your website is a blog, you can also submit it to something called a blog directory. You can find these online and submit your blog/s link to them. This will help people who are looking for a blog like yours find you. It may also help people with similar bogs why can link build with you find you.

If you have a business, you can do the same but look for something called company directories instead of blog directories. This would again help people who are looking for a business like yours to find you online and would count as a link in the eyes of Google.

Another thing that you can try is reaching out to the people and the sites that you link to. If you link to someone else, they may feel thankful and want to repay the favor by linking to your site. This is again not a reliable way to do link building, but it is at least worth a shot since writing a simple email does not take long at all.

Let's look into some middle-level link building strategies next. If you are a business and you already have customers, you can ask them to review you or to link to you online if they have a place to do so from. This is intermediate because you need to already have customers so you cannot really be brand new to your business and use this technique.

You could also consider sending whatever you make or sell to a blogger for free, and asking them to write a review in return. If your product goes to a blogger that has good SEO and a well-established following, it will be a link that will help your Google rankings for sure.

You can even consider contributing to sites like Wikipedia. Wikipedia is used often so it is a reliable and useful source to get a link from. It can also be edited by anyone, including you. This means that you can go onto Wikipedia, find a related topic to your site, and then you can actually link to yourself.

Next let's look into a few higher-level link building strategies. One thing that you can do is be the first person online to cover a topic or a news story. This is tricky because there are so many people posting online, but if you are truly the first poster you will likely get linked to from most of the posters that follow you.

You could also consider buying websites that already exist and have a good follower base. This would mean you would need to run two websites, but you can use your newly purchased site to link to the one that you want to raise in the search engine result rankings.

Next you could look into other sites and find one that is missing exactly what you have. You could then reach out to the owner of the site and point out what they are missing. You could show them that you have everything they need and they may think about linking to your site. Make sure that you are kind and come across as helpful in this process so that you do not upset the person you are reaching out to.

We have covered a lot of information on link building. We talked about what link building is and why it is so important. We looked into how you can get links, strategies that actually work for each experience level, and what you should avoid when trying to get linked to. We talked all about anchor text why it is important, and how to use it. We looked into link outreach and how to do it kindly and correctly. With this information, you will be able to be linked to in many ways and significantly boost your SEO. Remember this information and the tips we have shared in this chapter and you are sure to find success with link building.

Chapter Four: Social Media and SEO

In this next chapter, we are going to look into how exactly social media can affect your SEO. Social media is a fairly new thing that has been continuing to develop over the last decade, but it is something that almost every person uses today. Most people even spend time on it every single day of their life. If something has that big of an impact on society, it must be able to affect your search engine optimization.

The history of SEO and social media has been somewhat rocky. In the early days of social media, it was clear that it was a great tool for SEO. Then, in 2014, Twitter actually blocked Google from being able to use their analytics. Because of this, the importance of SEO and social media dies down quite a bit. Now, however, social media is extremely important to SEO again.

First, let's look into why social media is important to SEO. Google has started to realize that people love social media sites like Facebook, Twitter, and other sites. Because of this, they have been showing up in Google search results more and more. Google actually now considers these sites to be within their top one hundred sites to provide search results from. If Google puts this much weight on results coming from social media sites, it must impact your site's rankings somehow.

Let's figure out how this affects your site. First, SEO is for Google and social media is for interacting with the visitors of your site. Both are important, and both are actually related to each other as well. When you interact with the people from your site on a personal level, you are forming more of a relationship with them. This will make them want to read your information more often, which in turn will make you have more site traffic.

People are more likely to share the things that they love on social media than on other parts of the internet, because this is just how people live and interact in today's society. Because of this, your followers may share either your social media page or your actual website with the people they love on social media sites like Facebook or Twitter. If they do this, you will get new site visitors as well as more traffic from the older ones.

One of the ways that social media can help you the most is through content promotion. You can share any and all of the articles that you want to share with your followers. You do not need to worry about them needing to find your article through Google or SEO in this manner, but the extra traffic you receive of course still benefits your SEO anyway without much effort from you.

Social media also helps your brand awareness. When people are more aware of your company, blog, r web page, then more people will visit your site. This again helps your SEO. You can make people more aware of your site through social media because so many people are mindlessly scrolling through there already.

It is also important to know that your posts on social media are actually treated the same way that a web page is treated in the results of Google searches. This means that you should give as much importance to your social media posts as you do to your website, because they could be the things that show up in the Google search results first.

Let's look into some ways that you can use Facebook specifically to bring new visitors and traffic to your actual site. Facebook has something called a total count. When you share a post, this is the total number of likes, comments, and shares that your post receives. This exact number plays a huge role in where your post shows up in Google search result rankings. If your total number is high, your post has a much better chance at being seen in Google search results than if your total number was low.

Facebook is also a good link building tool. This is because people that you do not know will see the information that you share on your page without you even having to market to them. This may make some of your followers link to your content without you even putting in an effort to build links. This makes Facebook and great and easy tool that you can use to potentially raise your SEO.

Most of the time, Facebook is not a professional environment. Because of this, it is important for you to remember that even though it is just Facebook you still need to keep your content professional. This is important because again, your social media posts can show up in Google results. If an unprofessional post shows up on Google instead of your actual page, your SEO will be significantly lowered from the lack of site visits that you will receive.

Twitter now allows Google to see and use their information and the information posted to their sites by users again, so it is again a great tool to use for SEO. On Twitter, you need a lot of followers to show up in Google results. To get a large number of followers, try following a large amount of people. If you follow them, they are pretty likely to at least click on your page to check you out. If they like you and your page, they may even follow you back.

If you put high quality content on Twitter, you can use hashtags to help your intended audience to find your post. Make sure that your quality is good and that the content matches with what the hashtag says, though, so that your posts do not come across as spam.

It is also important that on Twitter, you fill out your biography section and that you fill it out in an accurate and exciting way. This will make more people interested in what you have to say because they will be interested in you as well. You should also put a link to your website in your biography section to help the people that like your tweets reach your actual page and give you even more traffic than you already have at the time.

There are other sites that can help your SEO as well. YouTube, for example, is a great one. YouTube is owned by Google, so their results show up high more times than not. Instagram, LinkedIn, and Pinterest can all be good SEO tools to use as well.

Next, let's look into something called social media analytics. Social media analytics are sites and tools that you can use to tell you how well you are performing on social media. They can tell you how many people are seeing your posts, interacting with it, and how to improve these numbers. They can tell you the best times of day to post to your specific group of followers as well as the posts that they enjoyed the most. This will help you to know your follower base well and understand what they want. You can then consider giving them more of what they want and less of what they do not want. This helps your social media followers to thoroughly enjoy their interactions with you and makes them much more likely to share your page and site with their followers, families, and friends.

Sprout Social is a good social media analytics tool. It can be tried for free for thirty days and then costs 99 dollars every year. It works with Facebook, Twitter, Instagram, and LinkedIn. This tool is nice because it allows you to see all of your social media accounts from different platforms all in one place. This can save you a lot of time and effort compared to having a separate analytic tool for every social media site that you have an account with.

Buzzsumo is a good tool to use as well. This tool does not look into your social media accounts. Instead it finds your actual website content on different social media platforms. It then tells you how these articles or this content is doing in different areas of the internet. This can be very helpful if you are looking into an article and not a social media account. Buzzsumo searches Facebook, Twitter,

Instagram, LinkedIn, and Pinterest. It also costs 99 dollars for every year that it is used.

Overall, it is easy to see that social media plays a huge role in your SEO and simply how people view and interact with the information that you post online, either on your social media accounts or on your website. Let's make a list of the things that you need to remember about social media and SEO.

- Social media post show up in Google results
- Social media sites increase viewer interactions
- Social media gains traffic for your actual site
- Make sure to have accurate and interesting social media biographies
- Facebook, Twitter, Instagram, LinkedIn, YouTube, and Pinterest can all affect SEO
- Social media analytic tools can help you manage your social media accounts and can help maximize the benefits coming from them

With this information and the tips and tricks that we shared in this chapter, you have every piece of information that you need in order to make your social media sites optimize your SEO.

Chapter Five: Web Analytics in a Nutshell- How to Measure Success

In the last chapter we touched on social media analytics, but in this chapter we are going to look into complete web analytics. We will talk about what Google Analytics is and why it is a good tool to use as well as how to use Google Analytics. We will talk about acquisition, organic search reports, segments, and other common web analytic terms. We will also look into call tracking, a powerful analytics tool for every business, as well as other web analytics tools.

First, let's figure out what Google Analytics is exactly. Google Analytics is a tool that tells you about the traffic that visits your site. It is similar to the social media analytic tools that we talked about above, but it simply works with your web page instead of your social media accounts.

Now let's look into why exactly you should be using Google Analytics to help optimize your SEO. The first reason why you should use this tool is because it is free. If something helps your SEO and does not cost you any money at all to use, why would you not give it a try? The fact that Google Analytics is free is a really great deal. Think back to the social media analytics tools that we talked about in the last chapter, for example. Both of them cost 99 dollars every single year that you use them. One came with one free month, but that is nowhere near as good of a deal as being a free tool for your entire lifetime. Since this tool does not cost you anything, you might as well at least give it a try.

The second reason why you should use this tool is because it is made by Google. Google is the company that created the tool, runs the tool, and provides you with your results. Why is this so important? Because Google is the exact company that you want your company to look good for. If this tool analyzes your website with Google's standards, it will surely raise your search result rankings in their own search engine. If you use an optimization tool made by the company who you are ultimately trying to impress, it is sure to be helpful.

Google Analytics is also a good tool to use simply because it works. It provides you with the results you are looking for when you use a web analytics tool. It gives you information about your site and the type of people who are viewing it. It can tell you your peak days and your peak hours as well as where your site is being accessed from on the internet. This information is very useful to figuring out how to improve your SEO, so you might as well take advantage of it.

Now that we know what Google Analytics is and why you should use it, let's look into how it works. It is important for you to understand how your SEO optimization tools work for a few reasons. The first reason why you should be aware of this information is so you can trust the tool. If you know how it works, you know that the information it provides is accurate and that its findings are typically very complete. You should also know how it works so that you can understand where the tool gets its results. If you understand how the tool gets the results that it gives you, you will be able to understand how to implement them better.

So, how exactly does the Google Analytics tool work? First, it works through the use of coding techniques. The URL to your website already uses coding, but Google Analytics puts many more codes into this as well. They also put more tracking codes into the coding inside the content of your web page. This cannot be seen by your site visitors so it does not affect your usability or readability. It does, however, track everything that the visitors of your site do. It even looks into the attributes of your site visitors and records them as well. These attributes include things like the gender, age, and even the interests of the people who view your web page.

Once the codes collect this information, they send it over to the Google Analytics page to be analyzed. They look into actions that every user does when they visit your site, how long each visitor spends in time on each part of your web page, how many times each separate page is viewed, how many buttons are clicked, how many times each video is viewed, and more. You can use this information to see what on your website is working well and what is viewed often by the visitors of your site, as well as what may not be going as well and what may not be being viewed very often at all.

Next, let's look into the information that Google Analytics provides back to you and how you can use it to benefit your site as well as your search engine optimization. The types of information that Google provides you with through the use of this tool are divided up into two separate categories.

The first of these two categories is User Acquisition Data. This information is all about the people who view your site and it is the information that Google has found out about them before they clicked on your site at all. It may tell you how old your viewers are, what gender they are, or what they like and what they dislike. User Acquisition Data can also tell you how these visitors got to your site in the first place. This data can tell you if the viewers clicked on a google result or if they came over through a link in a Facebook post.

This information is extremely helpful. It can help you to know what type of people are viewing your site. If you know what types of people you are writing to, you can consider catering your page more toward them instead of toward people who are not yet interested in your page. It is also extremely helpful to know how people are getting to your site. If people are mostly coming through Google search results, then you know that your SEO is in great shape. If no one is coming from Google searches at all, you know that your SEO probably needs a little help. If you see that many visitors are coming from Facebook posts, you can make sure you update your Facebook often to continue to allow more new site visitors to find you online, and so on.

The second of these two important categories of Google Analytics results is something called User Behavior Data. Instead of showing what your site visitors are like before getting to your site and telling you how they get to your site like User Acquisition Data, this category of information tells you all about what your site visitors do once they are already on your web page.

One of the first things that this tool can tell you about the people on your page is how long they stay on your page. This can tell you if people are enjoying your content or not. If most site visitors are only spending a few seconds on each of your pages, you may have some work to do to make your site more enjoyable If people spend many minutes on one particular page, you know that that is the type of content that they are looking for and the type of thing that they enjoy reading, listening to, watching, etc.

The tool can also tell you which page your visitors see first and which page they see last. This can help to show you which page your links are bringing visitors to and if this is a good first page to see or a bad first page to see. If it's the only page they view, it may not be the best first page. If they continue to click through all of your pages until the end, this may be a great sign. If people commonly stop viewing your content on a certain middle page, this may alert you to some sort of problem that they do not enjoy as well.

This tool can even tell you the order in which site visitors view your pages. This may be able to help you rank the interest levels of your different pages according to your specific group of viewers that you have for your web page.

User Behavior Data is interesting because it is an easy thing for you to change. You can look at the information that this tool gives you and adjust your site accordingly. If you do this, it is likely that you will quickly see results. It is much more difficult to change the results of your User Acquisition Data than it is to change your User Behavior Data.

The next thing that we are going to look into on the topic of web analytics and Google Analytics is something called organic search reports. Before we start going too deep into these details, let's learn what organic search results really are. First, it is important to understand that your website cans how up in Google search results naturally through good use of SEO tactics, or it can show up as a paid ad. Paid ad are not organic search results. Anything that appears naturally through SEO and is not paid for at all is considered an organic search result.

When you are using web analytic tools like Google Analytics, you should really be looking into your organic search results. You already know that paid ads will bring viewers to your site, but the long term goal is typically to get people to come to your site naturally without you having to pay for ads. In Google Analytics, you can look for just organic search report, which will show you how well your site is doing from a natural viewpoint. It will take out any type of data that comes through advertisements of any kind. When you view your website's organic search reports, you will be able to see what you need to do to improve your SEO if anything. It will help you to better understand the success of your website even if you have used paid advertisements in the past to promote yourself online. This tool will help you to see straight past those results so you can make sure that you have a great SEO that does the hard work for you.

We are now going to look into segments in regards to web analytics and Google Analytics. Segmentation in web analytics is when you look at the visitors that are coming to your site and then you divide them into different groups, or different segments. These segments could be something like first time visitors and returning visitors, for example. These segments help you to learn more about the people that are viewing and interacting with your site. They help you to see and understand what types of people are doing what types of things on your website.

When you understand the visitors that come to your site, you can better understand what they are looking to gain from your work. This can help you to format your site and frame your content to fit the needs of all of the types of people that you are virtually working for and working with.

There are many different types of segments that you can search for using Google analytics and other web analytic tools. One of these segments would be demographics. It can help you to understand where your readers are from and what areas of the world are interacting in which ways.

It may also help to do segments based on technology. This can help you to understand how many people are viewing your site from their smartphone and how many people are viewing your site from their laptop computer. You can then look into whether people seem to enjoy your site more in either of these settings or if they interact with your site more in either of these settings. This can then tell you if your site needs extra work in its mobile friendliness or if you should work more on how it looks when it is viewed from a computer screen.

You can also segment your viewers based on their behaviors. This can tell you if a lot of your views and interactions are coming from the same people over and over again or if your site following is made up of a large amount of people that do not visit your site very often at all. It can also tell you if the people who visit often interact more or if the new viewers interact more with the things that are on your web page.

Looking into the date that the people visited your site for the first time can be interesting as well. Are all of your visitors from when your site was made six months ago? If so, you may need to attract some new viewers. Did half of your followers show up on a random day in February? If so, look back to what you did that day in terms of marketing and definitely consider doing something similar to it again and again.

It may be helpful to look into your site visitors in groups based on how they found you online as well. This can help you to see if the people that mainly interact with your page content come from social media links or from Google search results. This can help you to determine if your site may need help in either of these two areas.

Enhanced Ecommerce can be a helpful way to segment site visitors as well. It can help you to see, if your site has things for sale, which of your interactions are coming from people who often purchase from you and which are coming from people who simply browse your site without ever making any purchases.

Now that we have looked into web analytics and specifically Google Analytics in such great detail, let's do a quick recap together. We talked about what Google Analytics is, why it is important, and how to use it. We looked into acquisition, organic search reports, and segments. Next, let's review some of the new web analytic terms that we have learned so far over the course of this chapter.

Acquisition: This is how people find your site. It's the way they reach your content, whether through Google search results, social media posts, links, or even just typing in your complete URL for your site.

Organic Search Report: This is a report that you can make through Google Analytics. It includes only your natural search results and does not include any visitors that come from clicking on paid advertisements.

Segments: When looking at web analytics, segments are groups that you can use to divide the visitors of your site by attributes like age, gender, site behaviors, and even their purchase history and many more.

Next, let's look into another important thing in web analytics called Call Tracking. Have you ever searched for a business because you needed to call them, and then been able to simply click on their phone number to complete the call? This information can be tracked with Google Analytics, and it is very important that you choose to take advantage of this. This is important because typically, people do not think about SEO when they receive phone calls. However, if you have a strong SEO and your phone number appears at the top of the result page, you are much more likely to get a phone call from someone searching on Google which of course can lead to more business for you. It is important to look into this information in Google Analytics so you know if it is working or if it is something that you need to improve on.

Finally, let's look into what types of web analytic tools are available online today. Of course, we already know about Google Analytics. This free told should definitely be used, but if you are looking for more than what Google Analytics offers, you may want to consider using a paid tool as well.

There are many different web analytic tools out there. It is up to you to decide which tool will benefit your business to the very best. The first web analytics tool that we will look into is called Adobe Analytics. It is easy to use and easy to understand, and it also provides real time data, not data that has been read hours ago in the past. This can be important when trying to optimize your SEO. It works very well, but it is extremely expensive. It costs many thousands of dollars every single moth if you want to use it. Because of this, it is really only a told that should be used by businesses that are already extremely rich and successful as well as businesses that know they will benefit from extensive web analytic help.

Angelfish Actual Metrics is a more middle ground product, but is still quite expensive as it adds up to over one thousand dollars each year that you need to pay to use its service. With Angelfish, you have the ability to measure the analytics of multiple sites at the same time, so it can be good for people that have more than one web page that they need to optimize. It also has the benefit of showing hidden visitors that google analytics does not have the ability to show to you.

If you are a beginner, Google Analytics is probably still the best place to start. This is because it is free so you are not wasting money if the web analytic tool you buy is something that is difficult to understand at first. Google Analytics also simply has most if not all of the features that beginners will want and need.

Overall, it is easy to see that web analytics are something that you really do need to know about when you are trying to optimize your SEO online. They help you to understand a lot more about the types of visitors that come to your site. They help you to see how people are finding your site, how much time they are spending on it, and how much they are interacting with you as well as many more helpful details. There are free web analytic tools as well as paid tools so there is a tool that is right for every type of web page and every different experience level.

Web analytics are important. We know that with this information, you will be able to understand them at least enough to start using them while trying to optimize your SEO. If you use web analytic tools in the ways that we have shared with you in this chapter, we are sure that your website and your following will benefit because of it.

Chapter Six: Troubleshooting Common SEO Problems

Sometimes, optimizing your SEO can be a frustrating process. Things can go wrong and you can lose the results that you worked so hard for. You can do all of the necessary steps and still not see the results that you so badly want to see. Because this can be difficult and frustrating, we are going to help you learn about common problems with SEO as well as how to troubleshoot each of these tricky issues.

First, let's look into what to do if your site in not showing up at all in Google's search results. The best way to check if your site is showing up is to type in your exact URL into the search bar. This should bring up a clickable link to your web page. If it does not, then your site is not showing up at all in the Google search results.

How can you fix this? It seems like a very complicated issue, but it actually is something that you can fix. You will want to check your site's Google search performance. It is likely that you need to greatly improve your SEO as well as other aspects of your web page in order to allow it to show up in the rankings.

Another reason why your site could be not showing up in the Google search results is because it is too new. Google needs some time to process and rank new sites, so its possibly that your brand new site may not be visible in Google search results for a little while after you create it. If this is the problem, there is not much that you need to do to fix it. In fact, there really isn't anything that you could do to fix this even if you wanted to. In this circumstance, you would simply need to give Google time. If your site is set up well and your SEO is at least off to a good start, your web page will show up in Google search results soon enough.

Remember those crawlers and spiders that we keep going back to? They could be the reason why you are not showing up in Google searches as well. If these spiders and crawlers cannot access your site, Google may not be able to see enough information to accurately display you in their search results. In order to make sure that these crawlers and spiders can do their job, you need to make sure that your website is accessible, that it has a good site speed, and that your site and URL are structured well. If you do not do these things, then the spiders or crawlers will have a very difficult time viewing your site if they can at all, and because of this they will not bring very much information if any back to Google. This will cause you to either not rank at all in Google search results or cause you to rank extremely low.

It is actually even possible that you are blocking these crawlers or spiders from reaching your page, and you may not even know that you are doing this. Some blog and website making software and websites like WordPress, for example, has an option that will completely block crawlers or spiders. If you accidentally checked the box that tells WordPress or any other site to do this, you will need to uncheck the box to make sure that spiders and crawlers are always able to access your site. After all, we know that they are extremely important.

It could also mean that you need to work on your keywords if you do not show up from Google searches. If your keywords are not placed correctly or if the keyword density on your site is not optimal, this could greatly affect your results in Google. It could also mean that the keyword you are using is not generating the results that you want. If this is the case, you would need to research new keywords and pick one that will perform better for you on your site.

If none of these situations apply, check your website's coding. It is possible that when you set your site up or when someone set your site up for you, it accidentally got set up with a "no index" tag. This type of tag would make your website not show up at all in certain Google searches. Check with the person who made your website to see if they could have accidentally done this. If you made your website, look into your coding for signs that you may have made a little mistake in this area that caused these tags to be added. The good thing is that as soon as your no index tags are removed, your site should show right back up in your Google search results.

If all of these things look good on your site but you still are not seeing it show up in Google search results, try to figure out if Google could have possibly taken down your web page. Google takes down sites everyday. They do this both if the site does not meet the Google quality guidelines and if it for some reason contains untrue or illegal information. If your site has been removed from Google, you will probably need to reach out to see what it was that you did wrong on your site. When you figure out why exactly your site was removed, you can go ahead and fix that problem. This should make your web page show up in Google search results fairly quickly once again.

Now that we know what to do if your site is not showing up in Google search results at all, let's move a little farther forward. Next, we are going to look into what you should do if your website is not ranking in the results for your own business name. Obviously, this is a problem that you do not want to have. It means that when people know about your company and they want to find it, they will either not be able to find it at all or they will at the very least have an extremely difficult time finding it. This will definitely hurt your site traffic and it will also probably hurt your complete business as well.

The first thing to do when this problem arises is to make sure that you are not checking your Google search results from your own browser. If you are, Google may be showing you different results because they know that you own your website. This could make your website come up as the top result for you since Google knows you visit it often, and this may make you think your SEO is in great standing when in all reality it needs a lot of help. It could also do the opposite. Googling your own site from your own browser could make your web page not show up in the results at all, even if you are searching your business name. This is because Google is giving you results for what you search for, they know that you already have access to your own website and the information that it holds. Because of this, they are showing you new information.

To get around this feature in Google, you will want to open up an incognito, or secret, tab on your computer or mobile device. When you do this, Google will show you what everyone else in the world sees when they search the name of your site instead of just what Google shows to you. This can help you to get a clear and correct image of how Google portrays you to random searchers on the internet at this time. If you see what everyone else sees, you will probably find out that your web page actually is showing up in Google search results. You may even see many ways in which you can improve your SEO and get your rankings to move up higher on the list.

Another thing to look into if your site is not showing up when you search for your own company name is to check on your SEO tactics. Make sure that your keyword usage is in good shape. Make sure that your site is readable and usable. Make sure that it has a structure that actually makes sense. Look into your analytics and search for reasons why your website may not be going as well as you think it is going. If it is not showing up in very exact Google searches, it probably needs quite a bit of formatting help before it will be ready to be published again. If you follow the tips we have shared with you in this book, however, fixing your website should be a pretty quick and painless process.

Now that we have looked into what to do when you cannot find your website on Google in their search results, let's look into what you can do when you do find your website but it happens to be at a much worse ranking than it was when you checked in on it the week before. There are many reasons why you could see a Google ranking drop, let's look into what they are and what you can do if they happen to you and your website.

The first thing that could make your rankings drop significantly is if you receive a Google penalty. Google penalties happen when you do not follow along with the Google quality standards. You can tell that this is the problem with your site if you type in different searches with multiple different keywords, and your site is significantly lower than it used to be for every single search that you do. If you happen to find that you have received a Google penalty, first you should figure out why you received it. You can then go ahead and fix the problem. This should make your rankings go back up to where they used to be in just a little amount of time.

Your Google rankings could also drop when another search result, one of your competitors, moves ahead of you in the rankings. This can mean that they somehow improved their SEO to the point that they show up higher in the results than you do. This one is a little more difficult to come back form as it takes some time, but you will need to work on your SEO to once again surpass this competitor. Consider looking at the site of your competitor. What are they doing to improve their SEO? How are they tackling the ever important task of link building? It is obvious that what they are doing is working well, so you may even want to consider copying what they are doing. They are showing you that their tactics are giving them the results that you want and need, so you might as well try these tactics for yourself.

On Page issues can cause your site's ranking to drop as well. These problems could be something as simple as broken links. If your google search result rankings seem to be dropping from on page issues, consider carefully reviewing all of the content on your site as well as the features that your site has. If you can find an error, fixing it will probably help you to move back up to where you were and where you want to be in the search results.

Another reason why your search result rankings could have dropped is because there was a recent change to Google. Google has many updates and is constantly trying to improve. Because of this, they often change the algorithms that they use to rank search results as well. If you can find no reason why your site should be dropping based on how it looks or how your competition looks, check in with Google. If they have recently done an update, you will have found your issue. You can also try to stay ahead of Google updates as well. If you know when the updates are coming, you can adjust your site so that its ranking never actually gets to the point where it will drop.

The last reason why your site may drop that we are going to look into together is classed a Google Flux. This Google Flux is something that you have no control over. They are also unpredictable, so you will never be able to tell when they are going to happen. They make your site drop for no reason. Luckily, this is not a permanent drop and your site will be back at the ranking that it belongs in within a few days. If you can find no reasons for your site to drop based on your web page and based on your competitors, and you also see no signs of a Google update, it is probably a Google flux. Try not to worry and check back in a few days. Most likely, your search result rankings will be back to normal.

These are the most common problems that you may face that lead to your Google search result rankings dropping. When you see them, you can look back to this chapter so that you are able to help your rankings return to normal. With this information, you should be able to troubleshoot any search engine ranking issue that comes your way.

If you are still having a hard time with your SEO, however, you may just feel like you need some advice or help from a professional. Professional help is always a great thing to have, but of course it can be extremely expensive. Luckily, there is a tool that allows you to get free SEO help from a professional online.

This tool is a website called WiSEO. On this site, you can type in a question that has to do with any part of SEO. When the professionals on the website see your question, they will take the time to answer your question. They do not do this for money of course because their service is free. They do this simply to help you in your journey with SEO. They are a great resource to keep on hand.

Overall, with the information in this chapter, you should be able to solve any search result ranking that comes your way. If you come across a problem that you are not able to solve, you can always reach out to the experts at WiSEO for free, professional help.

Chapter Seven: SEO for Local Business

Typically, your SEO helps your site to show up in search engine results from anywhere in the world. When you use local SEO, however, you can promote your site or your business to people who are near you. In this chapter we are going to learn all about local SEO. We will talk about why using SEO is important, how you can rank high with local SEO, and local SEO search ranking factors. We will discuss how exactly you can go about getting started with local SEO. We will learn about building citations and building reviews. We will also look into supercharging local SEO with photos and videos as well as a local SEO ranking checklist and other essential resources.

One important thing to note is that in order to use local SEO to its best ability, you need to have a proper physical address. If you do not have an address that you can publicly use for your site information, you will not get very much out of using local SEO. However, if you do not have a physical address that you can use in the area, you can still use some local SEO. In this case, you would simply need to write a lot of content about the area you want your readers to be from. If you do this, your result should still show up in Google's search results when people are looking for something in that specific area.

Now let's look into why exactly you should use local SEO. Local SEO is extremely important because it simply provides great results. It is a tool that can build your SEO quickly. It is also just another way to build your search engine optimization. If you've already done all of the tips and tricks we have talked about in this book so far and you want your website to still rank higher in Google's search results, local SEO has another new list of tips and tricks that can help you achieve this.

Local SEO is extra important if you are a small business owner with only one or a few in-person locations. It is important in this situation because you want your site to show up in the results of local searchers. If you have a plumbing company in Pittsburg, you probably do not care if you show up in the search results of people who are looking for plumbing in San Diego. You only really need to show up in local searches. In cases like this, you can focus mainly on local SEO tactics while you are building your site.

Now that we have looked into what local SEO is, why you should use it, and how to rank high with it, let's look into the local search ranking factors.

Knowing this information will again help you to improve your local SEO simply because you know the basis of what makes you rank high or low or somewhere in between.

One great tool to use in local SEO besides writing about your specific city of interest is writing about the towns that surround that city. People will drive away for things that they like or things that they want to experience. Because of this, if you also market to people who live in surrounding areas, you may get into their search results as well. If you have good content on your site that interests your visitors, they may choose you even over businesses that are physically closer to them.

Another really cool thing about local SEO is that it does not have to contain only online pieces to help it succeed. If you tell people in person about your business, they may go home and look up your website online. If you have a billboard or put up flyers, people may see your name and search for you specifically on Google. If you have customers that are happy with your services, they may tell their neighbors and local friends about you as well, which would once again lead to people looking you up online and bettering your SEO.

For local SEO, you will also want to do something called "Google My Business". This is a Google service that helps businesses to share their own details. It allows you to go onto Google's site and edit facts about your site or company. It will ask you to add all of your locations and to verify your business. This will allow your site to show up higher in the searches of local people because Google knows that your company is real. Google My Business also lets your customers log into its site and rate and review your business. If you have good reviews, your site will show up higher in local Google. If you have poor reviews, your site will show up lower in the search results. When you get reviews, you can even go a step further by responding to the comments that are left by your customers. You want to be very friendly in these comments. You also want to make sure that if you receive poor reviews you do not respond to the comments with a grudge or any other type of negative tone. If you get a good review, sincerely thank the person who left it. If you get a not so good review, sincerely try to help improve the negative experience the person had with your business. When you are interacting with customers online, Google suggests that you treat them like a friend. This well help to show that you care and will improve the way that local people see your business. Even if potential customers see bad reviews online, they will also see you trying to help solve the issues. This will help how people see you and your company which will in turn improve your business as well as your local SEO.

Another great tool for local SEO is Facebook. As we mentioned earlier in the book and as you probably already know, Facebook is everywhere. Not just is Facebook everywhere, but it seems like almost everyone in the world is on Facebook as well. Because of this, it is extremely important that your business is on Facebook and that it is represented well. Since people are on Facebook so much, it is pretty common for them to use it to find local businesses when they need something from them. They can do this by asking for recommendations or by simply searching for what they need in the search bar. If they have heard of your company before, they can look your Facebook page up to learn more about your business as well. Facebook also allows its users to review your business, so you can help your local SEO by responding to these comments nicely just like we talked about doing for the Google My Business reviews.

A simple way to optimize your local SEO is to just add your city and state to your title. When you do this, Google is able to tell easily which local searches you should be entered into. The title of your site is important in the factors that Google looks into for your SEO. Because of this, if your title includes both your business name and your city and state, it should show up well in the searches that you need it to show up in the most. This is also a good thing to do because it is so easy. It takes basically no time or effort and can make your Google search result ranking much better in the area where you want to advertise yourself the most.

You can also look into other local web directories. These are sites that list business information like yelp.com. These are good resources because they are simply another thing that can show your business in the local search results, and they can also have a link to your actual website. As we learned earlier, links like these are the best way to improve your SEO. The more directory sites you put your business information and site links into, the better your local SEO will be just because your name will be more visible in the search results and because of the link building that this does for you.

Let's look a little closer at these links that we have been talking so much about. In local SEO, the best links are people who refer your business or company on their site. This may be even better if the person referring you is also local and if they happen to have great local SEO. These links are still very powerful to your own SEO. They help your Google search results rankings greatly and direct people to your site from other places on the internet.

Even though you are working on getting local results here, you cannot forget about using the pieces of typical, widespread SEO. You still need to make sure the content of your site is as good as it can possibly be. It needs to be readable and usable so that it is able to be enjoyed by the visitors that come through. It needs to have a good structure and a well-made URL so that Google can read it and those spiders and crawlers can easily access your information.

In local SEO, you also need to remember keywords just as much as you need to do so in regular SEO. Make sure to use keywords both for describing your business as well as mentioning where you are from so that you are able to show up easily in the Google search results for both of these things.

You also need to remember that prominence is used in Google's local SEO decisions. When you have a perfect site with great SEO from every side, you may still be underneath that name brand company in your town that also has locations in every other town. If this happens, do not be discourages. This is simply one of the ways that Google chooses to rank results. If you keep working hard on your local SEO you may pass them up in the results someday. If not, remember that if people want the best option for the service or product that they need, they will probably look at and compare the top few choices. Because of this, you will likely still get a lot of business even if you lose the number one spot to a chain company location nearby.

After reading through all of these ways to rank high in local search results and the ranking factors of local SEO, you should be able to optimize the SEO of your local business site fairly easily. If you use all of these tips and tricks, we are sure that your local SEO will be in great shape.

Next, let's look into how to get started with local SEO. We already know what to do, but let's make a step by step game plan so that you can do this in as easy of a process as possible. We are here to help you the best we can!

1. Look at your title, does it include your city and state? If not, add it. This simple step will help you greatly in your local SEO success.

2. Make a Google My Business profile. Add and verify the information for your business. Bookmark this page so that you can come back to it to respond to any comments or reviews you happen to receive.

3. Make a Facebook page. Use this page to display business information, share posts that

may interest your intended viewers, and interact with your customers and potential customers. After all, most people are on Facebook today anyway. You may as well use it as a tool to share your business with them.

4. Add your business to local directory sites. The more times your business shows up in search results, the more times it will be seen. Plus, you can use this as an opportunity to link to your website as well.

5. Link Build! Ask other local sites and companies to link to your page and consider returning the favor and linking to their page as well. This is the one thing that makes a huge difference in your SEO.

6. Advertise around your city. If people see posters or billboards with your company name, they are likely to google it and look for your website.

7. Be friendly. Log back on to your Google My Business and Facebook profiles. Interact with the people you are reviewing you in kind and helpful ways.

8. Make sure your address is listed on your site.

9. Look at your website. Make sure the content is relevant. See that your site is readable and usable overall. Look at your keyword

placement and density. Look back to all of our regular SEO tactics and put them to use as well.

With these nine tips, you should not only be able to get started with local SEO, but you should be able to excel in this area as well. We hope this information causes your local Google search result rankings to skyrocket and that this leads to more business for your local company as well.

Now that we know how to use and benefit from local SEO, let's learn about something called citation building. First, it is important to know and understand that a citation is any type of mention of your business on the internet. These can be mentions of the name of your business, your address, your phone number, or any combination of the three of these pieces of information. A complete citation is called a NAP. NAP stands for name, address, and phone number. When a citation has all of your information because of the NAP, people online can find your business very easily either online or even in person.

The cool thing about citations is that even if they do not link back to your business's website, Google stills treats them the same way that they would treat a link. Remember how important links are? Because they are so important, this is a hugely helpful tool in local SEO. The more times your NAP, or really any part of your business, shows upon the internet, the higher it ranks in the Google search result rankings. Some of these citations can even include links to your website. This would make an even more powerful SEO boost for your company site.

There are two different types of citations in local SEO. One type of these is called a structured citation. These are from local directory sites like yelp.com that we mentioned earlier in this chapter. They can also be from sites like Facebook.

Unstructured citations are any other types of sites that show your business information but are not necessarily a listing for your company. These could include things like when your business is mentioned and reviewed in a blog and the writer includes your information so that people can try out your business as well.

Both of these types of citations help to verify your business to google and their search engine results team. It shows that your business is real because it is being mentioned in multiple different places on the internet by many different people. It also adds to your prominence level since you are mentioned more times online overall.

One thing that you really need to be careful about when it comes to citations is that your different citations round the web are consistent. They all need to have the correct information, so this should make them each have the same information as well. If the sites have incorrect or different information, this not only confuses your potential clients, but it hurts your local SEO as well.

Now that we have looked into building citations, how to do it, and why it is helpful, let's look into building something else. Next we are going to talk about building reviews, how you can build them, and why it is important to do so.

As we already know, reviews are comments from people who have used your products or services in real life. They are the honest opinions of your customers. They can be great, horrible, or somewhere in between. Reviews are made so that people know what they are getting before they decide to pay for your product or for your service. They ensure that people are getting high quality experiences from what they purchase as well, since if the products or services are bad someone is sure to tell the world about it soon enough.

The more good reviews you have, the better you show up in Google's search results rankings. This is why it is important for you to build up your reviews. Working on building reviews can be a fast way to boost your local SEO.

Next, let's look into how we can boost our reviews. The first way that we can boost reviews is pretty simple. When people visit our business, we can ask them to go online and review their experience with our products or services. If you ask a person to review you, they may actually do it. Of course it never hurts to ask someone for a favor, so this is any easy step that you might as well take to help your SEO improve at the local level.

Another thing that you can do to encourage reviews is to place signs inside your business that encourage people to review their experience online. This eliminates you having to ask every customer for reviews. It also helps customers to notice that a simple review is something that would really help your business in a concrete way.

You could also consider getting the email addresses of your customers when they pay at your business. If you do this, you can send them an email after asking them how their service was and asking them if they could please review you online. You could even provide a link in the email that the customer could click on in order to be brought to a site that they can leave a quick review on.

You could even try offering an incentive for the people that choose to leave a review. You could put their name into a monthly drawing or even give them a coupon for a percentage or a dollar amount off of their next service.

With these tips, you should be able to continue to get more reviews. The more reviews you get, the better your local SEO looks. Even if asking for reviews is not your favorite thing to do, remember that it is making a huge difference in your SEO.

There are a couple other things that we have not yet mentioned that make a huge difference in local SEO. The first of these two things is photos. When your site includes pictures, people are more likely to notice your business. Pictures are the main thing that is seen on social media today and it's easy to notice and recognize right away. If you have photos online, people will notice and interact with your content much more than if you did not have photos on your site. Because of this, something as simple as a picture of your storefront can benefit your local SEO in big ways.

Videos are the second of these two simple but strong tools. Videos are popular right now and most people like to watch them when they are surfing the web or scrolling through social media. Watching a video takes less effort than reading or researching, so viewers are more likely to learn all about your business in this fashion than they are to click onto your site and read through all of the pages. Because of these factors, videos can really supercharge local SEO.

In this chapter, we have learned all about local SEO. We have learned that it is just like SEO but for local searches and we have discussed why it is so important to use it. We have learned the ranking factors for local SEO as well as how to rank high with it. We created a list together of how to start this process, talked through citations, reviews, and even the great benefits of citations and reviews. After reading all of this information, you should be able to have great success with your local SEO.

Chapter Eight: The New Meta: JSO-LD, RDF's Microdata, and Schema.org

This chapter is where we start to get a little more technical with our SEO talk. Do not worry, however, because we will be sure to talk through these things in a way that is easy to understand. Even if the title of this chapter looks like a strand of letters that you have never seen put together before, by the end of this chapter you will feel confident in your understanding of each of these things.

In this chapter, we are going to be looking into something called the meta. The meta description, or meta tag, is the small description that Google shows underneath your title and website link in their search results. Meta simply means meta data. Meta data is information about the content of your site. There are different types of tags that you can use on your site for the small description that shows up in Google search results, and we will be looking into each one of these types over the course of this chapter.

First we will continue discussing metatags as a whole. Meta data helps SEO, which is why you should know what it is as well as how you should go about using it. They help SEO by letting Google know what the content of your web page is actually about without Google having to look through your entire site.

First, you will want to figure out if your site is using metatags. To do this, right click on your page and when the menu box pops up, click on "view page source". When you do this, the page will show you the metatags if they are being used. If meta tags show up, definitely take the time to look into them. It is important that you understand the metatags that your own site is using. If your metatags are not relevant to your site or if you are not getting the traffic you would like to see and you want to try something new to increase it, consider changing your metatags.

There are four main types of metatags that people commonly use and that show good success rates in most cases. The first type is called Meta Keywords Attribute. This meta tag is a list of keywords that you want your site to show up in the google search results for. The keywords should also be used in your content of course, but putting them in a metatag can help as well. The second type is called a Title Tag. This metatag shows the title of your site and can help you to show up in the results when someone searches for the title of your page on Google. The next type is called a Meta Description Attribute. This type has a short description of the content of your page within the tag. The last main type is called a Meta Robots Attribute, and this helps those spiders and crawlers know exactly what to do when they get to your site.

Each of these types of metatags have their own time and place to be used. However, some are much more useful than others. For example, Meta Keywords Attribute is not as useful as it used to be. This is because people used to just type in random keywords that they knew would generate a lot of search results even if the words had nothing to do with the content of their site. Google figured this trick out, and now does not put as much weight on Meta Keywords Attribute because they need their search results to always be relevant and helpful to the people who are using their search tool online.

Meta Descriptions Attribute is a lot more helpful. With this tool, Google still puts quite a bit of weight on what you right as your description. This makes this type of meta tag a good tool to use to make your site show up in the searches that you need to be visible in.

Meta Robots Attribute is helpful as well since it tells the spiders and crawlers what to do with your site. This also helps you to show up in the search results that you need and want to be in the most.

Title tags are the most helpful of all of the types of meta tags. These have a high power when looking into the google search results. They're also something that can be seen by people when they are looking at the Google search results. These are actually the things that make the titles of links to sites show up in Google's results list.

Even if you are a beginner, you can use meta tags to better your search engine optimization, or your SEO. You can look up the information or simply eve read through this chapter of our book. It should help you to understand meta tags enough to implement them on your own site. If you are still struggling with meta tags, you can use online tools that are made to help you with them.

Next, we are going to look into some newer ways to better your site that are similar to meta data but that may actually work even better. The first thing we are going to look into is called JSON-LD. JSON-LD is a linked data tool. It allows for people to click on one site and then be brought through multiple other sites. It is easy to implement on your own site and it is easy for your readers to read as well.

The next tool we will look into is called RDFa. RDFa is a tool that stands for resource description framework in attributes. RDFa works with attributes of sites and tells what these attributes are through extensions to more sources of data. This should be capable of providing Google with even more information about your site than typical meta tags can do.

Microdata can be used to describe yourself as well. This is a tool that simply gives names to different pieces of the content on your site to allow it to show up in different Google search result lists. For example, if you write one article about cooking on your blog but you typically write about horses, your cooking article may need to show up in a different google search. This is where microdata can come in handy because it can make that happen for you. This is a tool that is nice for people with multiple businesses or who write a blog about more than one topic.

Schema.org is another tool that can be used. This tool can add a list of different vocabulary words to your site's tags. This can take different pieces of your site, like content, ratings, or your location, and add them all into tags for you website. This can help you to show up in more Google searches while keeping you results in relevant places at all times.

The last tool that we are going to look into is called Facebook Open Graph. This is the tool that allows you to log into many different websites across the internet using your Facebook log in. This is an easy way for people to log into your site and also is an easy way to see and study the types of visitors that are coming to your site. When you know who is visiting your site, you can consider writing specifically for that type of crowd to gain more followers and visitors and increase your SEO. It also allows you to use the Facebook plug ins. These include the like button, comment feature, and the ability for viewers to show your page to their personal Facebook page. This can help spread the word about your website faster than many other methods that we have talked about so far.

Overall, it is clear that there are quite a few tools that can use your SEO. We have covered the best and most helpful tools in this chapter. These tools may seem difficult to use at first, but once you learn how to use them it will become easier and easier. Like anything else, once you practice with these tools you will become better at them and they will provide you with better results. Also, typically tools that require some extra thought and effort are tools that can help you more than things that are easy to use. Everyone would use these if they were easy. Because of this, if you learn how to use even one of these tools you can have the opportunity to really boost your SEO and set yourself apart from your competition.

Chapter Nine: Where to Start

Now that we have covered these helpful tools, let's spend some time learning how exactly we can start using them. We know that these tools can be a little tricky and somewhat complicated when you first look into them. Because of this, we are going to help you get started. We want you to succeed and we believe that by the end of this chapter, you will be able to start using these tools with ease.

First, let's look into schema.org. Why should you use this tool? As we mentioned before, you should use this tool because it can greatly benefit your SEO. Let's look into what schema.org is in more detail and discuss why exactly it is a tool that you should be using for your site as soon as possible.

First, it is important to know that schema.org is something that people around the world contribute to. It is a joint effort to provide success to every person who knows about and uses the tool. This in itself is a great reason to use schema.org because it is like a community. It is a place where you can support others in their SEO journey and it is a place where they will support you as well.

Another reason to use Schema.org is because it can be used with all of the other tools that we have talked about so far. It is simply a tool that generates vocabulary to provide you with SEO success in the area of microdata. It can be used along with JSON-LD and RDFa, which we talked about in the previous chapter. Both of these tools provide great success and schema.org can make that success even greater.

The first thing that you need to do in order to start using and benefiting from schema.org is familiarize yourself with tags. Luckily, we have already covered this information in the last chapter so you should already be able to check this step off of the list. If you do not yet feel comfortable with tags, consider going back to the information that we covered in the last chapter and reviewing it once again.

Next, you will want to understand what schema markup is. This is simply the rich vocabulary that you use in your site and in your tags. This vocabular is then able to tell google what your content actually means instead of google just seeing the words that you write for everyone to see.

You can then select what type of information you want to mark up on your website and the schema community will help you with the process of finding the right vocabulary to use.

Now let's look into how to get started with JSON-LD. First, let's remind ourselves on why this site is so useful in the first place. JSON-LD makes the data and information on your website show up in a way that is easy for spiders and crawlers to read. This benefits your SEO greatly with just a little bit of effort from your end.

How do we get started with JSON-LD? To start with this tool, you will need four types of keywords. The first type of keyword is the Schema. This keyword is for version control. The next type of keyword is the ID, or identification of the site. The next keyword includes the description and the title. The last keyword includes the type.

You then add properties to each keyword. This helps the spiders and crawlers to know exactly what you mean by each keyword, which helps you to get into the exact Google search results that you want to be in.

You can continue to go deeper into the properties of the keywords including things like product names and even prices. Everything that you add will narrow down your search results to get exactly where you want to be more and more.

Overall, JSON-LD is just a way of controlling how the spiders and crawlers read your site's data. It's a way of controlling how you show up in Google search results. If you are not showing up in the ranking spot you want to be in or if you are showing up in search results that don't fully fit your website's purpose, JSON-LD is a great place to start the process of getting your site to where you ultimately want it to be. With the details we just covered, you should be able to use this tool pretty easily as well.

Next, let's look into Facebook Open Graph. Before we look into how you can use Facebook Open Graph, let's look into why exactly you should be using it. This tool is good to use because it simply provides you with so much information. It tells you what types of users are visiting your site and what content they enjoy the most. It also helps greatly to spread the word of your site. It allows your site visitors to share your content on their personal Facebook pages, which in turns makes sure that your content is seen by many more people. It shows on Facebook how many likes and shares your content receives, so people may be more willing to click on it when they see that it has been interacted with by many other people. It also allows for comments. You can use these comments as reviews. If you have some extra time you could even respond to these comments to help grow your SEO and site visitor appreciation at the same time.

You can add Facebook Open Graph to your website through the use of tags. The tags should show what the content of your website is about so that it can be found by people who are either looking for that type of content or at least people who are already interested in that type of content. This also again helps Google to know what your site is about so that it can sort it into the right search engine results.

After adding the tags you want, you will have to change the html code of your website. When you change this code to include Facebook, the open graph program will be added to your site. You can then add a like button to your page with an iFrame or with a Java Script SDK placed in your tags.

You will then need to add Open Graph meta tags. The meta tags that are required are og:title, og:type,og:Image, and og:URL. If you want to, you can also add the optional codes which are og:description, og:site_name and og:app_id. Of course, the more tags you add the better off your results will be, so it is a good idea to add these extra and optional tags if you have the time and ability to do so.

Once you have completed all of these steps, your site should be all set to work with Facebook Open Graphs. Just these few simple steps will bring you large amounts of information that you can use to optimize your site, and it will also bring your site way more exposure than it would get without the use of Open Graphs.

Schema.org, JSON-LD, and Facebook Open Graph are all great tools to use on your site. Now that we have covered how to get started in each of these areas, you should be able to implement these tools into your own site. They may seem complicated at first, but with the information you have learned in this book and a little bit of practice, we know that you have the ability to succeed with these great SEO tools.

Chapter Ten: Final Powerful SEO Tools

We have covered a lot of information in this book so far. We started by talking about what SEO means, and now you just finished learning some of its most complicated pieces. In this final chapter, we want to share with you some final tools that will help you greatly to have the best SEO that you can possibly get.

First we will look into research tools for SEO. We looked a little bit into keyword research earlier in the book but just to refresh your memory, keyword research helps you to come up with keywords and it also helps you to understand the power behind each different keyword. They help you to see how keywords are performing on the internet today before you decide to use them on your own site.

Wordstream has a free keyword research tool. This tool lets you pick a niche and gives you lists of suggestions to use for the actual keyword within that niche. It can be used for thirty free searches and you get a seven day free trial after your thirty free searches are used up, so you can actually use this helpful site at no cost for quite a long time.

Soolve is tool that is always free. It shows you the keywords that are typed in most often on a variety of different search engines when you give it a topic that you are interested in. It is a great tool for coming up with keywords that you may not have been able to think up on your own.

Ubersuggest is an extremely fast and easy to use tool. It is also free. When you give it a topic, it instantly gives you a huge list of keywords that you can look through and choose from. It is a great tool to use if you want something that is easy, free, and something that does not take much time from your already busy schedule.

Ahrefs Keyword Explorer is a great tool for a more advanced version of keyword research. It has a huge number of keywords in its system and it adds new words to its database every single month. This means you can keep getting new results from this tool if you need to use it on the same topics more than once. The topics it has now are probably enough, though, since it has close to one million keywords in its database. It looks into clicks, clicks per search, and return rate when deciphering which keywords are the best. It works with three types of keyword ideas including autocomplete, questions, and suggestions.

SEMrush Keyword Magic Tool can be helpful as well. It has less keywords in its database, but still plenty to help you find what you need. It shows you a graph of how much the keywords have been used over the course of the last year. If you are a person who learns well from visuals, this is a good tool for you to choose.

Google AdWords Keyword Planner is of course a good research tool for keywords as well. It is a part of Google so it helps a lot with your SEO in Google's search results specifically. This tool is great to use because it's just easy. It is simple to use and provides great results.

Next, let's look into optimization tools. Optimization tools are of course important because the whole point of SEO is to optimize our search engine results. It's even in the name of the thing we are looking into (SEO). These are tools that help to make sure you show up high in the rankings of the Google search results.

One of the best optimization tools is a tool that we have already talked about in this book called Google Analytics. As we talked about earlier, Google Analytics shows how your site is performing online. It shows who is visiting your site, how long they are staying, what they are clicking on, and what else they are interacting with. It can tell you the peak times for visitors on your site and the type of people who are following you in categories based on things like gender and age. This information can help you to see how your SEO is doing and it can also help you to get to know your audience. If you know your audience, you can cater to them and make the number of viewers you have continue to grow.

Google Page Speed Insights is a good optimization tool as well. This tool checks both your site speed and the usability of your site. As we learned earlier, both of these things are very important factors when trying to better your SEO. This tool even gives you ideas on how you could possibly improve your site speed and the usability of your web page. It tells you what to change as well as what to keep the same with its user experience scores.

Moz Local Listing Score is a great tool to use when you are looking into your local SEO. This tool allows you to see where you stand compared to other local sites in terms of SEO. Based on the information you find with this tool, you should be able to optimize your SEO even more. You can continue doing what you are doing if you are at the top. If there is competition that is ranking above you, consider looking into their SEO tactics to see what is working so well for them. You can change your game plan to match or outscore theirs after gathering this information.

Even just simply using the incognito window on your computer's web browser can be a great optimization tool. When you use the incognito window, you can see where your site actually stands in the Google search. You cannot do this with a typical browser window because Google knows that you own your own site, so they will make it show up high in the results for you. This does not mean that it shows up in the same place for everyone else. When you use the incognito window, you see what everyone else in the world sees when they find your web page. Based on your findings with this tool, you can look back into your tactics on your you can better optimize your search engine result rankings.

Next, let's look into tools that can help you with link building. We know that link building is extremely important and that it can allow you to build your SEO faster and easier than any other tactic that you can ever do. We also know, however, that it is a challenging thing to do. Because of this, these link building tools can be extremely helpful.

The first tool we will look into is the social media site Instagram. Instagram is actually a great tool to use to find links. This is because many businesses and blogs promote their sites on Instagram. This is also because the site owners typically take a very personal presence on this site and they tend to be very friendly with their followers. To try to get links with this tool, you will want to follow people that have similar businesses or similar blogs to you. You could also follow small business owners that live in the same town as you are that live in a town nearby. When you follow these people, they will probably follow you back. You will then want to begin an online relationship with them by commenting on and liking their posts. Once you feel you have built a strong online relationship with them, you can ask them to link to your site within their content sometime. This is not a tool that is guaranteed to work, but it does work often so it is definitely worth a try. Plus, you'll be adding exposure and content for your site while you work on the relationship so even if they say no, your work will not be a wasted effort.

Another great link building tool is Moz Link Explorer. This is a free tool that allows you to see where on the internet your site and your content is linked to from. When you can see where on the internet people are able to click and be redirected to your site, you are able to judge how you are doing in the link building department. If you have a large amount of links coming to you, you are probably doing pretty well. If you have no links, then link building is definitely something that you will want to start spending more time on when you work on your site.

Ahref's Backlink Checker is a great tool as well. We looked into another one of Ahref's tools earlier on in this chapter, and this tool is just as high quality as the last one that we looked into. This tool allows you to pick any website, copy and paste their URL into the search bar, and figure out where they are linked to from everywhere on the internet. This can be a great tool to use if you are wanting to know how your competitors are getting their link building from. You can copy and paste the URL of your competition's website into the search bar and see where their links are coming from. You can then use this list of links as a list of ideas on who you can contact in your link building journey. You can try contacting the same people that your competitor did, or you can try contacting similar pages and people. You know that your competitors link building is working, however, so you will definitely want to do something like what they are doing since they are finding the success that you are searching so hard for.

Another really helpful tool in look building is a site called Guest Post Tracker. This site keeps a running log of websites across the internet that are currently accepting submissions for guest bloggers. If you use this site, it takes away some of the time that you would have had to spend researching which blogs you should reach out to. It also gives you the peace of mind that at least when you reach out to these people, you already know that guest blogging is something that they at the very least consider. You are not going to annoy them or offend them by asking to a be a guest blogger on their site, because they say that they are actively searching for and accepting guest bloggers. This site does cost money to use, but it is just a onetime fee of 99 dollars.

Lastly, let's look into tools that can help you with your web analytics. As we learned earlier in this book, these tools help you to understand who is viewing your page, when they are viewing your page, and what they are doing once they get to your page. These tools can be helpful because they help you to get to know your audience so that you are able to consider catering specifically to them. Typically when you know your audience, you are able to help grow your site viewers quickly.

The first tool that is extremely helpful with web analytics is Google Analytics. We already mentioned this tool so we won't look into it in detail again. We will just mention that this tool works well because it is run by Google and Google also runs the search results that you are working so hard to stand out in.

Another great web analytics tool is Woopra. Woopra is a tool that shows the tracking of real time analytics. This tool is unique because it not only lets you track your site visitors, but it lets you interact with them as well. If you are looking to get to know your site visitors on a more personal level or if you have a lot of time to be online while people are checking out your site, then this tool is definitely for you. Woopra has different plans ranging from free to a few different price points. The higher priced options of course come with more capabilities than the free and lower priced options.

Clicky is another helpful tool when it comes to web analytics. It does the typical web analytics tracking of people that visit your site, but it comes with another feature as well. Clicky allows you to view the actions that people are doing live while they are visiting your site. For example, you could choose a viewer and watch what they are seeing on the website. You can pay attention to what they click on and how much time they spend on each page. You can actually experience this type of tracking instead of reading it through data. This is an interesting twist and can make web analytics a little more fun. This site is also free to use, which is a huge added bonus.

Kissmetrics is another great web analytics tool. This tool again watches the visitors that come to your site and analyzes their actions. The cool thing about this site, however, is that it stores the data that it finds, It then takes this data and analyzes it, looking for patterns and behavioral changes that happen over time. This can help you to be even more aware of what is happening with the visitors of your site.

Overall, it is clear that there are many sites we can use to better our SEO. We only mentioned a few of the best tools in this book, while in reality there are hundreds of tools available online that are made to help you maximize your SEO. There are more research tools to help you get the best keywords. More optimization tools to ensure your website is in tip-top shape, more link building tools to make a difficult process a little bit easier, and more web analytic tools so that you can understand your site visitors even better. If you use any tools at all, they will help you to improve your SEO. You can use one tool from each of these sections or you can use multiple tools to receive advice and help from multiple different sources and varying points of view. You can stick with the first site you try or you can try every one of these tools until you find one that you love using. You can even read through this list and decide that you do not care for any of these powerful tools and that you would rather find your own different tool to find online. We know that you now have enough knowledge on SEO to make educated and informed decisions on what is best for you and for your own site. We hope this chapter gave you a good idea of where to start with powerful SEO tools and that you are able to use these sites to benefit your SEO and your business and website overall.

Conclusion

We have covered a lot of information together in this book. When we started out, we were discussing the most basic topics from what SEO stands for to how Google works. We then moved on to talking about Google ranking factors and how to rank well in the search engine results.

We looked into keyword research and we learned that this is the most important step of search engine optimization. We talked about finding keywords, how to tell if a keyword will bring you success in SEO, as well as how to use keywords and where to place them in your content.

We then talked about all of the different things that you need to be aware of when you are working on bettering your SEO. We mentioned things like on page SEO, structure, site load speed, duplicate content, usability, readability, and mobile support. We talked about how to accelerate traffic to your site and how to be featured in Google's featured snippets in order to receive more traffic to your site.

We discussed link building in detail and talked about how this is the most powerful tool that we have in SEO. We learned how to get others to link to our site as well as what to do and what not to do when it comes to building links.

We covered social media sites like Facebook, Twitter, Instagram, Pinterest, and LinkedIn. We talked about why these sites are important for SEO and how exactly you can use them to benefit your overall SEO.

We looked into web analytics and what it can do for us. We learned why this tool is important and how we can use it. We talked about terms like acquisition, organic search reports, segmentation, and more. We learned that this told helps us to measure the success of our site and shows us how we can improve as well.

We learned about problems that may arise while we work with our SEO like not showing up in google searches or dropping our rankings significantly. We learned what causes these problems as well as how we can fix them when they do happen to occur.

We talked about local SEO, how it is different from normal SEO, and why it is important for your business. We learned how local SEO is ranked in google search results as well as how to improve these rankings through things like citations and reviews. We talked about the difference that can be made through something as simple as phots or videos.

We learned a few of the more complicated SEO procedures including JSON-LD, RDFa, Microdata, and Schema.org. We talked about how to get started using each of these told and learned the benefits that each one carries.

We ended by covering many more tools that you can use in your SEO journey including research tools, optimization tools, link building tools, and web analytics tools.

You may have been a beginner to SEO when you started this book, but by now we know that you are ready to succeed in this area. You have all of the knowledge you need and every tool you'll want to have a great SEO for your website. We wish you luck on your SEO journey and we are glad that we were able to help you get to this point.

Made in the USA
Middletown, DE
26 August 2019